MODERN REALISM

ACCORDING TO FRITZ

The Oil Paintings of Fritz VonderHeiden

EDITED BY
LAWRENCE KNORR

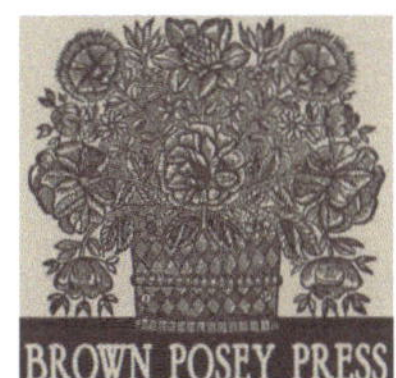

Mechanicsburg, Pennsylvania USA

Published by Brown Posey Press,
an imprint of Sunbury Press, Inc.
Mechanicsburg, Pennsylvania

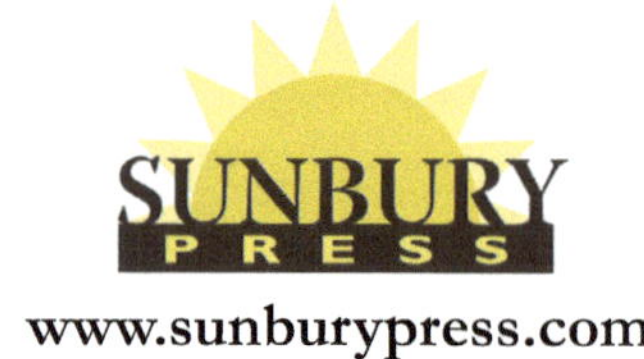

www.sunburypress.com

For information about special discounts for bulk purchases, please contact Sunbury Press Orders Dept. at (855) 338-8359 or orders@sunburypress.com.

To request one of our authors for speaking engagements or book signings, please contact Sunbury Press Publicity Dept. at publicity@sunburypress.com.

FIRST BROWN POSEY PRESS EDITION: February 2020

Publisher's Cataloging-in-Publication Data
Names: Knorr, Lawrence, author | VonderHeiden, Fritz, artist.
Title: Modern realism according to fritz : the oil paintings of fritz vonderheiden / by Lawrence Knorr.
Description: Revised trade paperback edition. | Mechanicsburg, PA : Sunbury Press, 2020.
Summary: Catalog of 127 oil paintings by artist fritz vonderheiden of camp hill, pennsylvania.
Identifiers: ISBN 978-1-620064-49-8 (softcover)
Subjects: | BISAC: ART / Individual Artists / Artists' Books. | ART / History / Contemporary (1945-). | HISTORY / US History / Mid-Atlantic.

Set in Bookman Old Style
Designed by Lawrence Knorr | Cover by Lawrence Knorr | Edited by Lawrence Knorr
All artwork by Fritz VonderHeiden

Product of the United States of America
0 1 1 2 3 5 8 13 21 34 55

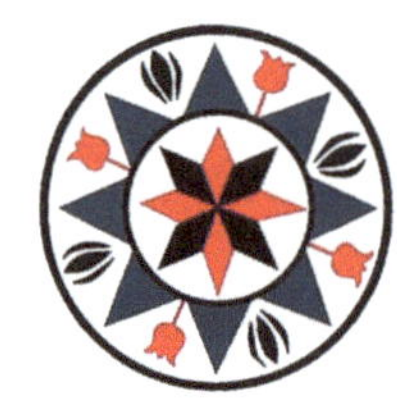

Continue the Enlightenment!

Table of Contents

"I dream of painting and then I paint my dream."

Vincent Van Gogh

"The secret to so many artists living so long is that every painting is a new adventure. So, you see, they're always looking ahead to something new and exciting. The secret is not to look back."

Norman Rockwell

A Little Bit About Fritz

"And since geometry is the right foundation of all painting, I have decided to teach its rudiments and principles to all youngsters eager for art."

Albrecht Dürer

Fritz VonderHeiden was born in 1934. Art has always been his first field of interest, but he also had an early tendency towards science and math, so when the time came for education beyond high school, he opted for engineering instead of art, and graduated from Lehigh University in 1956.

The art was put on hold for a long, long time, although he did do an occasional painting or two. After several years of employment in private industry, he took a job with the State of Pennsylvania and was employed in the Department of Health and the Department of Environmental Resources as an analytical chemist for fifteen years. After leaving the state job, he worked for several more years with local engineering firms as a mechanical draftsman. Finally, after retiring fully, he began spending most of his time doing oil paintings, which has continued to the present.

Fritz grew up in Pottsville, Schuylkill County, but left Pennsylvania after Lehigh and worked a year in New York City, several more in New Jersey, and then went to Charlottesville, Virginia, where he earned a master's degree at the University of Virginia. He came to Harrisburg in 1964 and has lived since then in Camp Hill, with his wife of 42 years, Marilyn.

His work has been exhibited in several local galleries, including ones in York, Selinsgrove, Carlisle, Hagerstown, and Baltimore in Maryland, and even once in Washington, D.C.

In 1990, one of his paintings, *Station Break*, appeared in the October issue of *Modern Maturity* magazine as one of the winners in a competition for senior citizens.

In 2008, he received the "Best of Show" award at the York Art Association's annual juried competition, for the painting, *Verifying Gravity*.

Fritz's favorite American painters are Edward Hopper, Winslow Homer, John Singer Sargent, and George Bellows. His favorite European painters are Johannes Vermeer, Vincent Van Gogh, Claude Monet, and Albert Marquet.

Scenes of Harrisburg

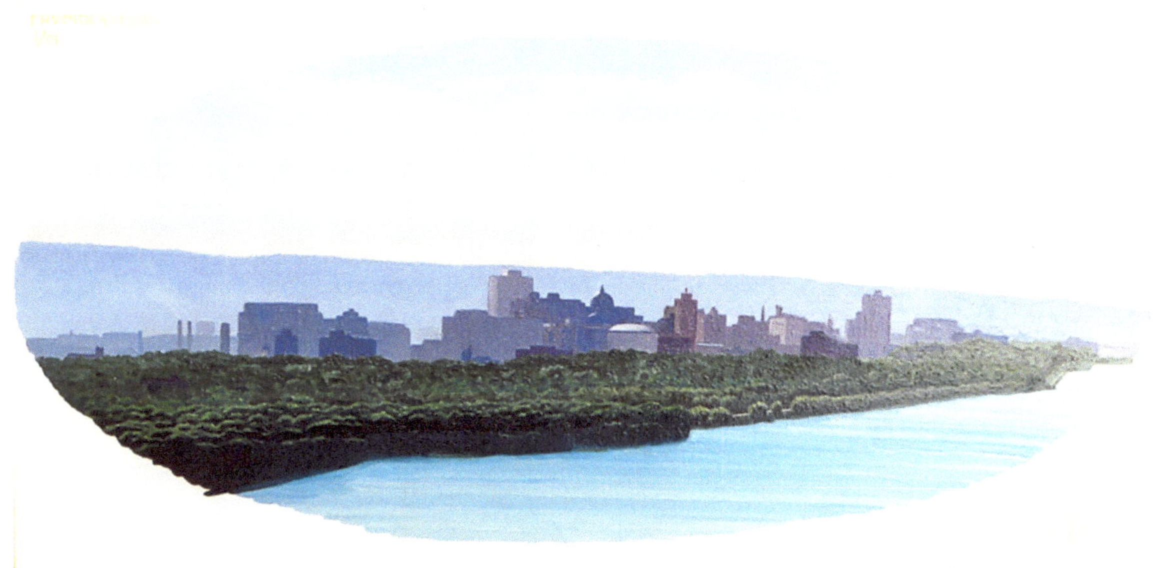

River City. 1991

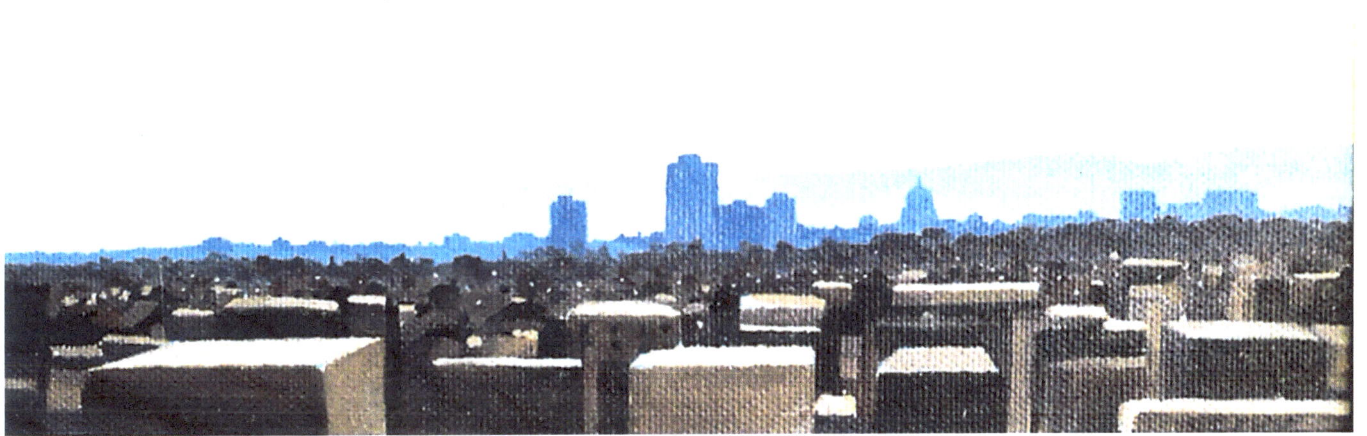

On a Clear Day, 1992

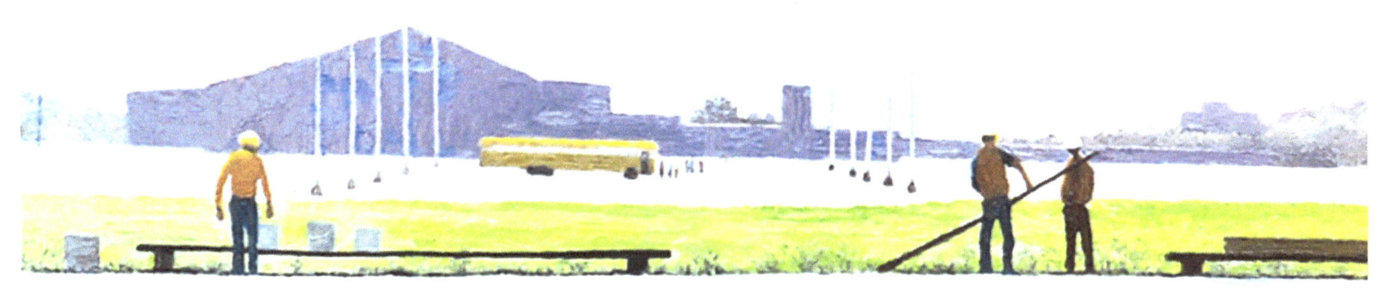

Workmen Near the Farm Show Building, 1993

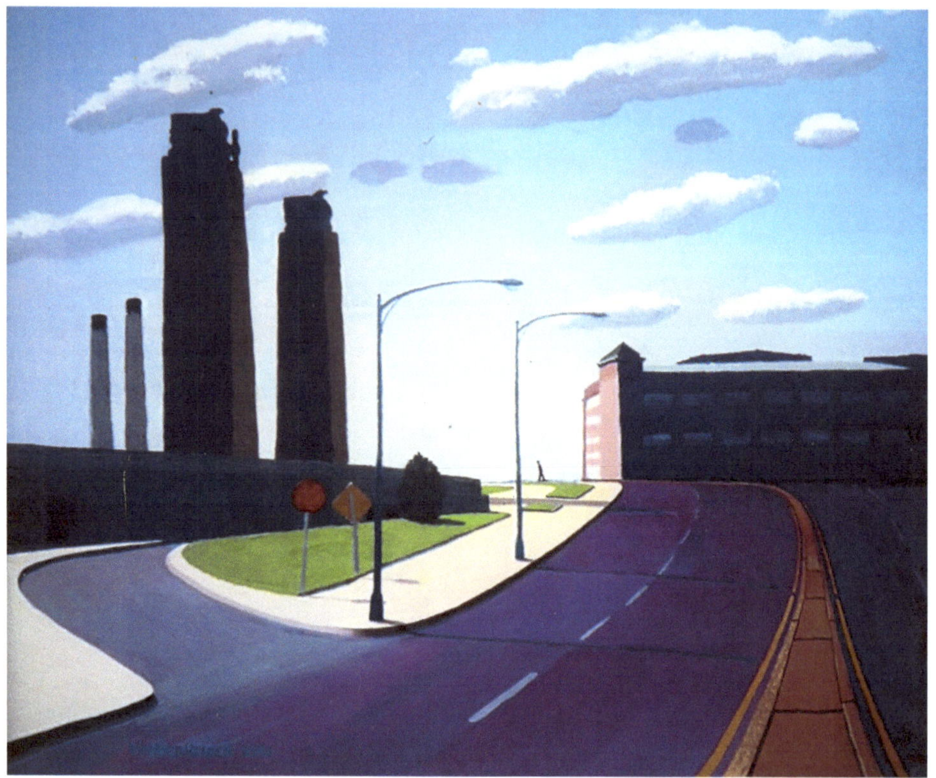

Building by the Bridge, 1991 (front cover image)

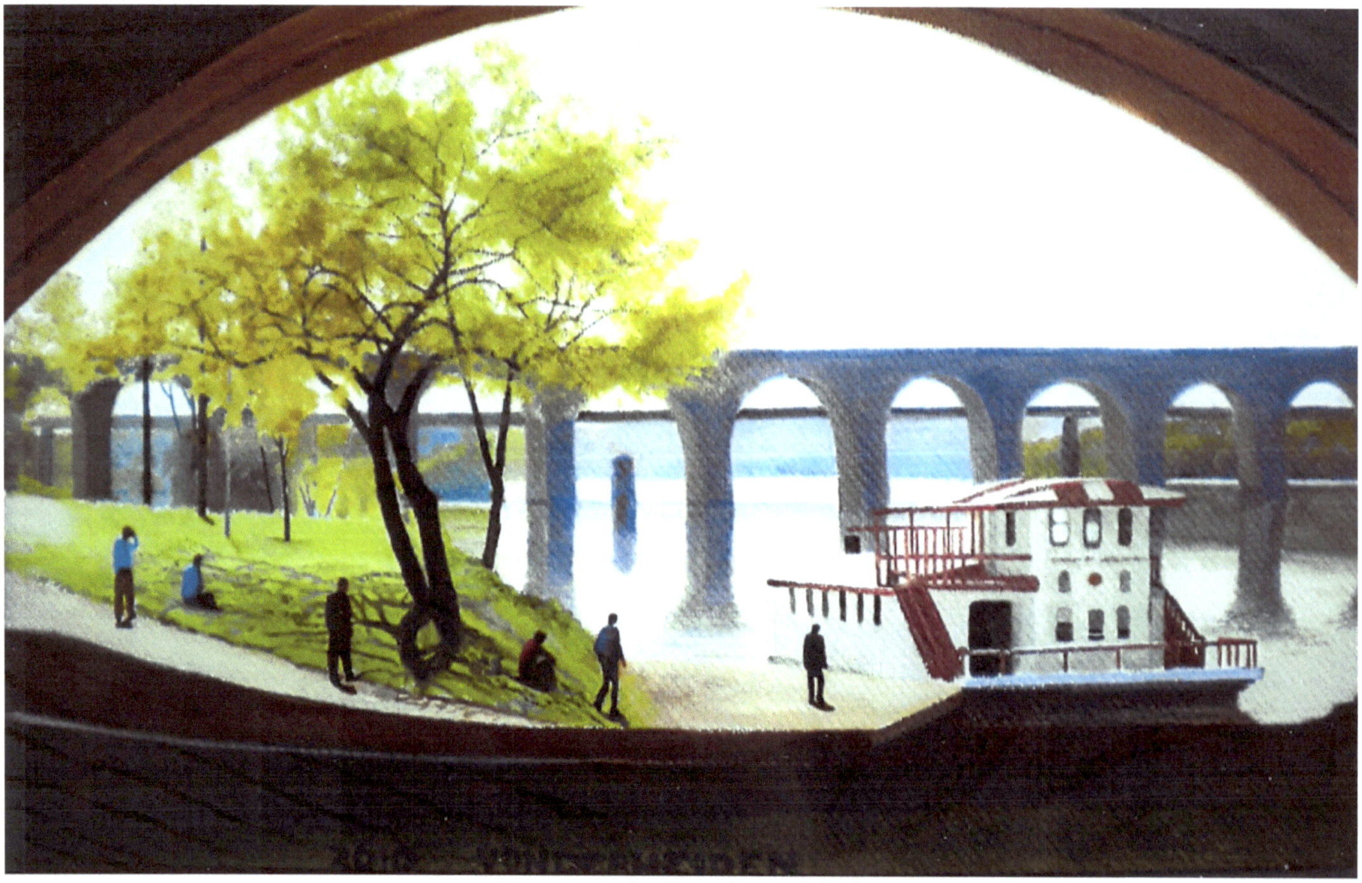

Return to the Riverboat, 2010

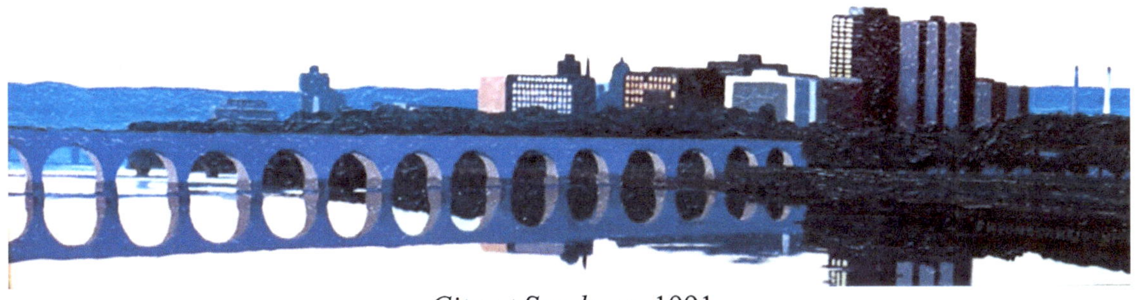

City at Sundown, 1991

Morning in the City, 2005

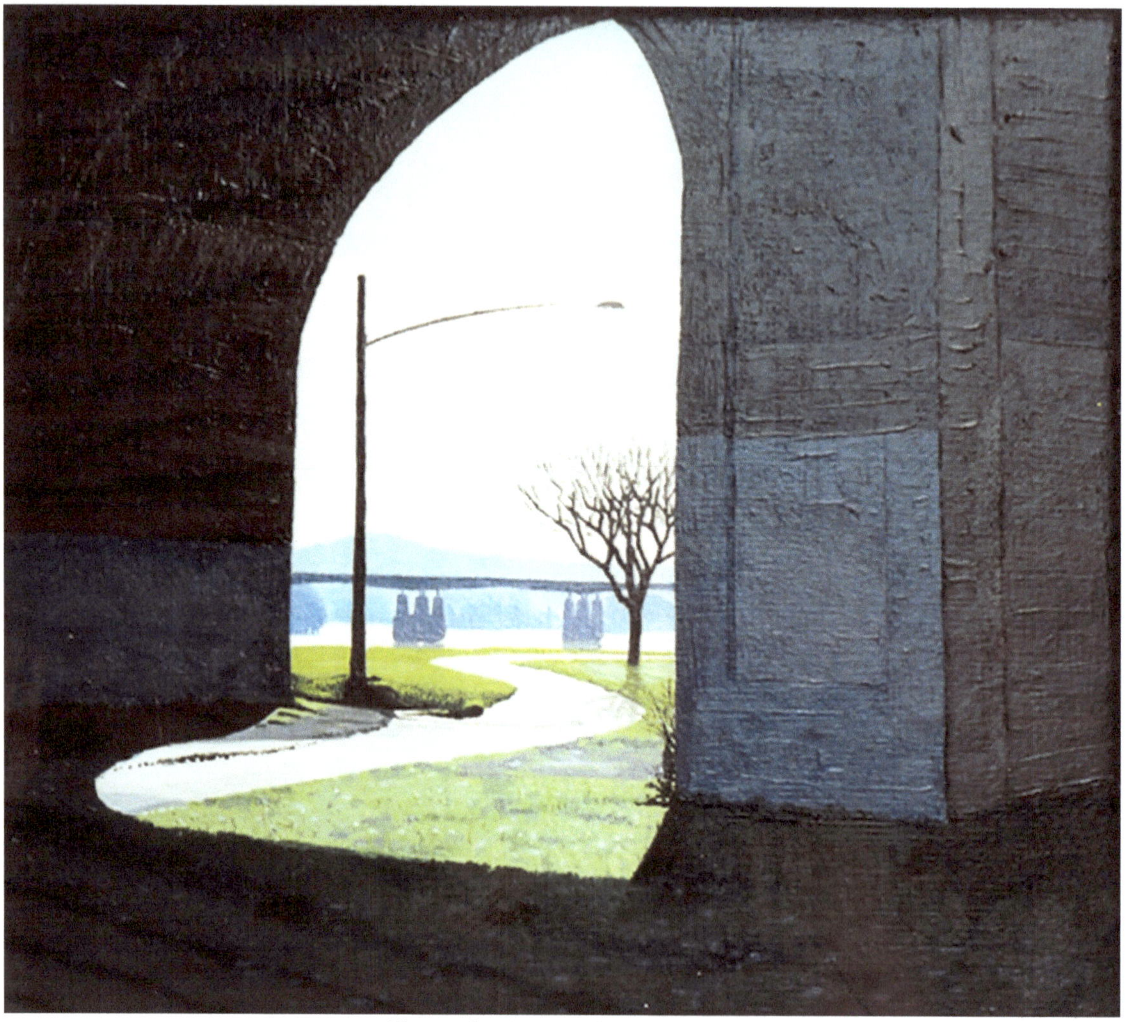

Along the Susquehanna, 1989

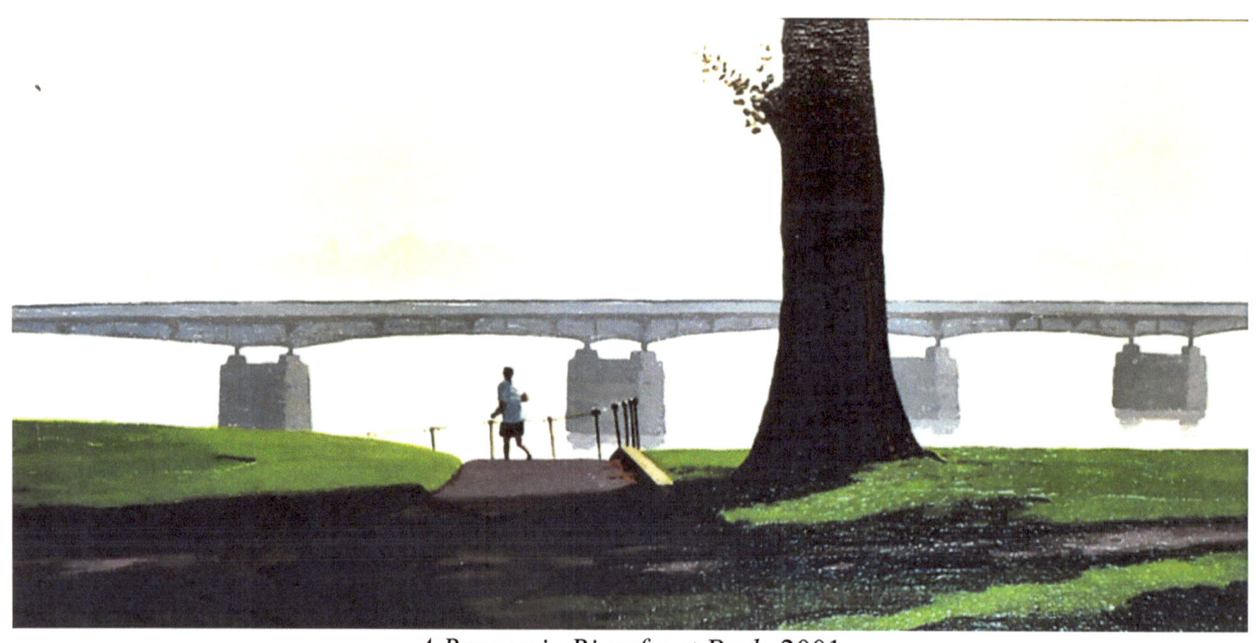

A Runner in Riverfront Park, 2001

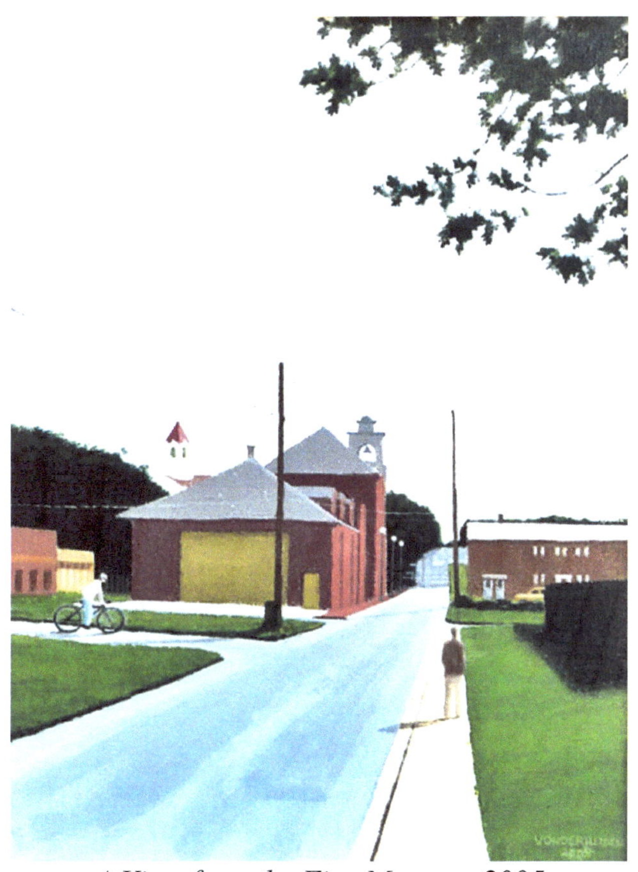
A View from the Fire Museum, 2005

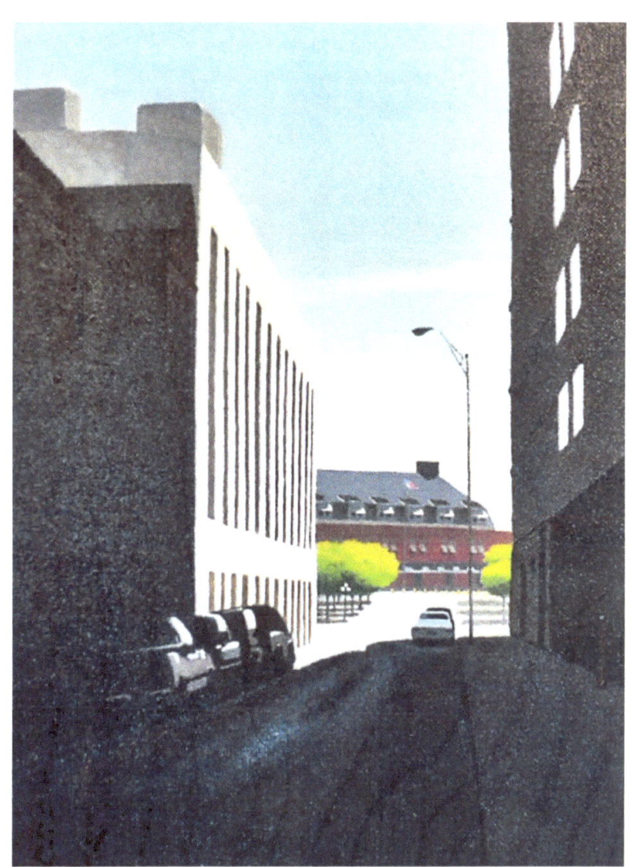
A View of the Transportation Center, 2005

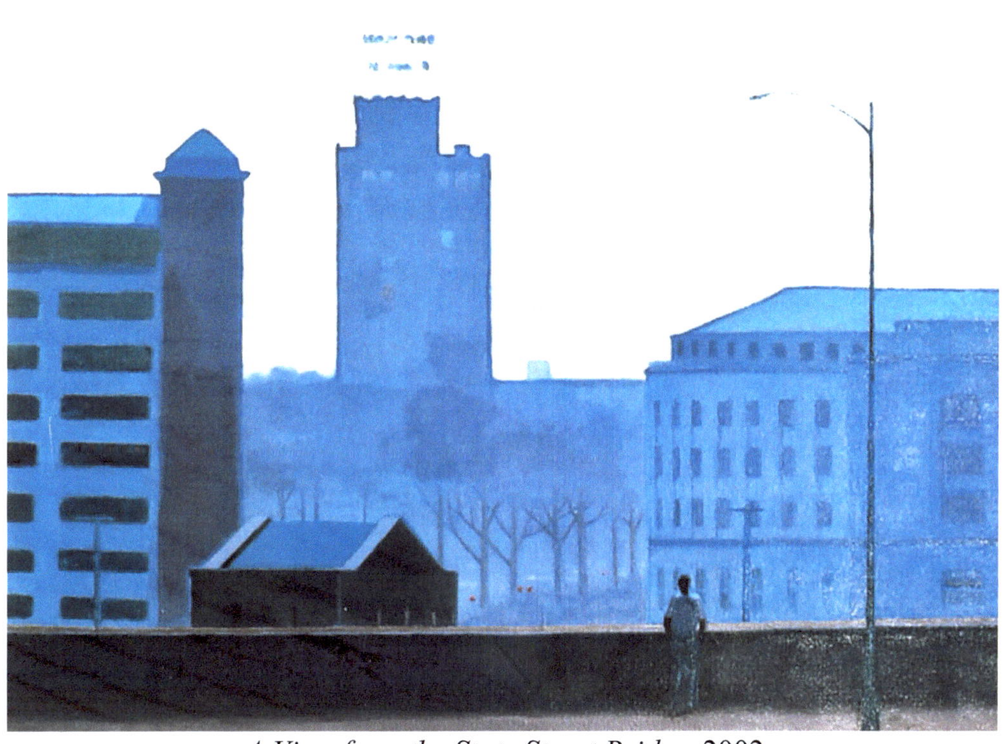
A View from the State Street Bridge, 2002

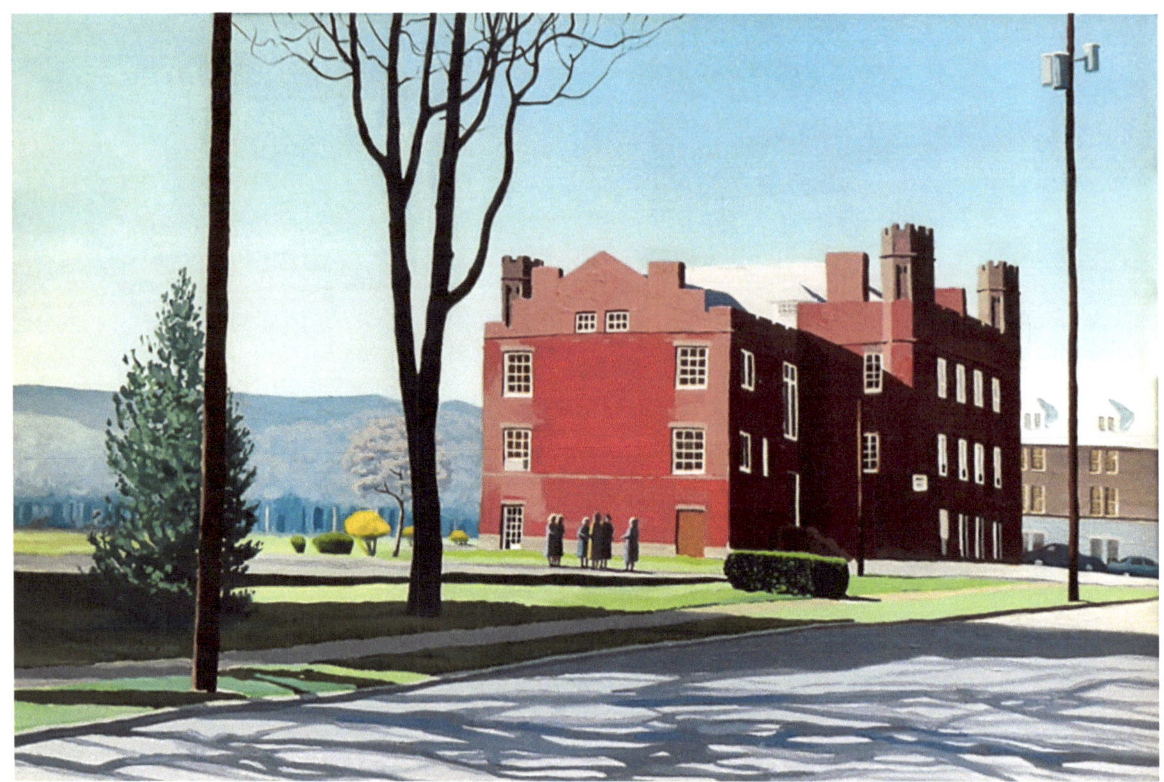

Hunter Hall, 1990

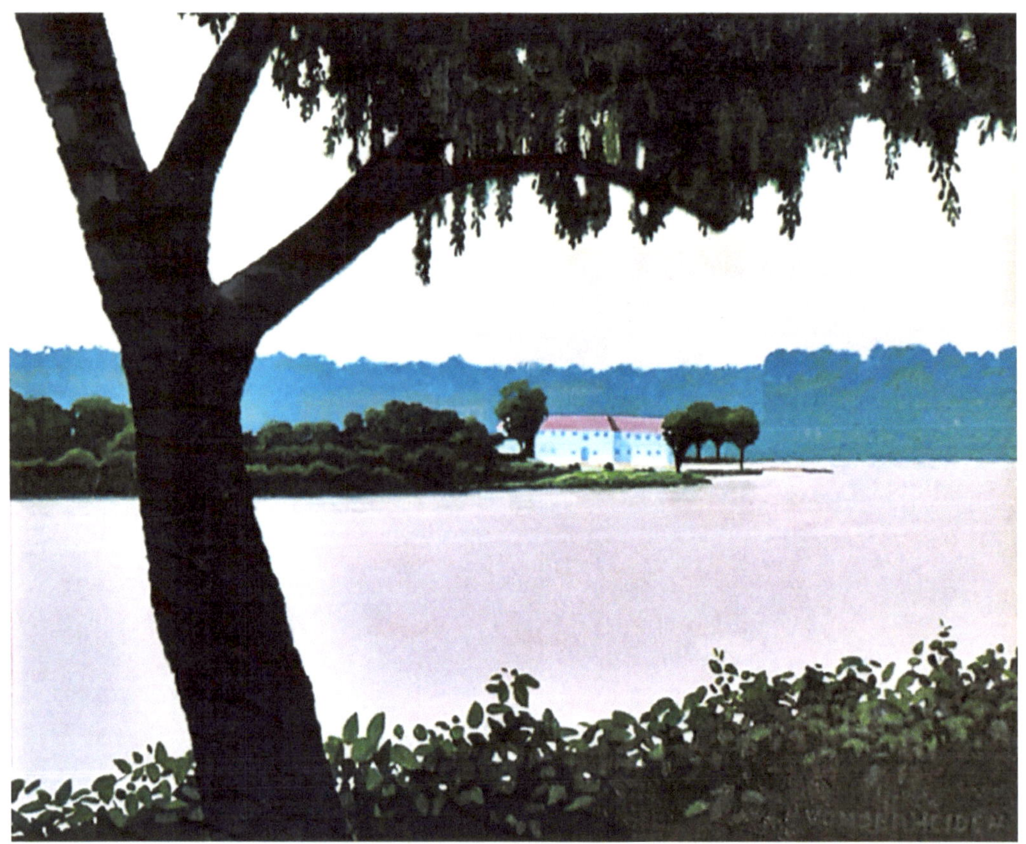

The North End of the Island, 2007

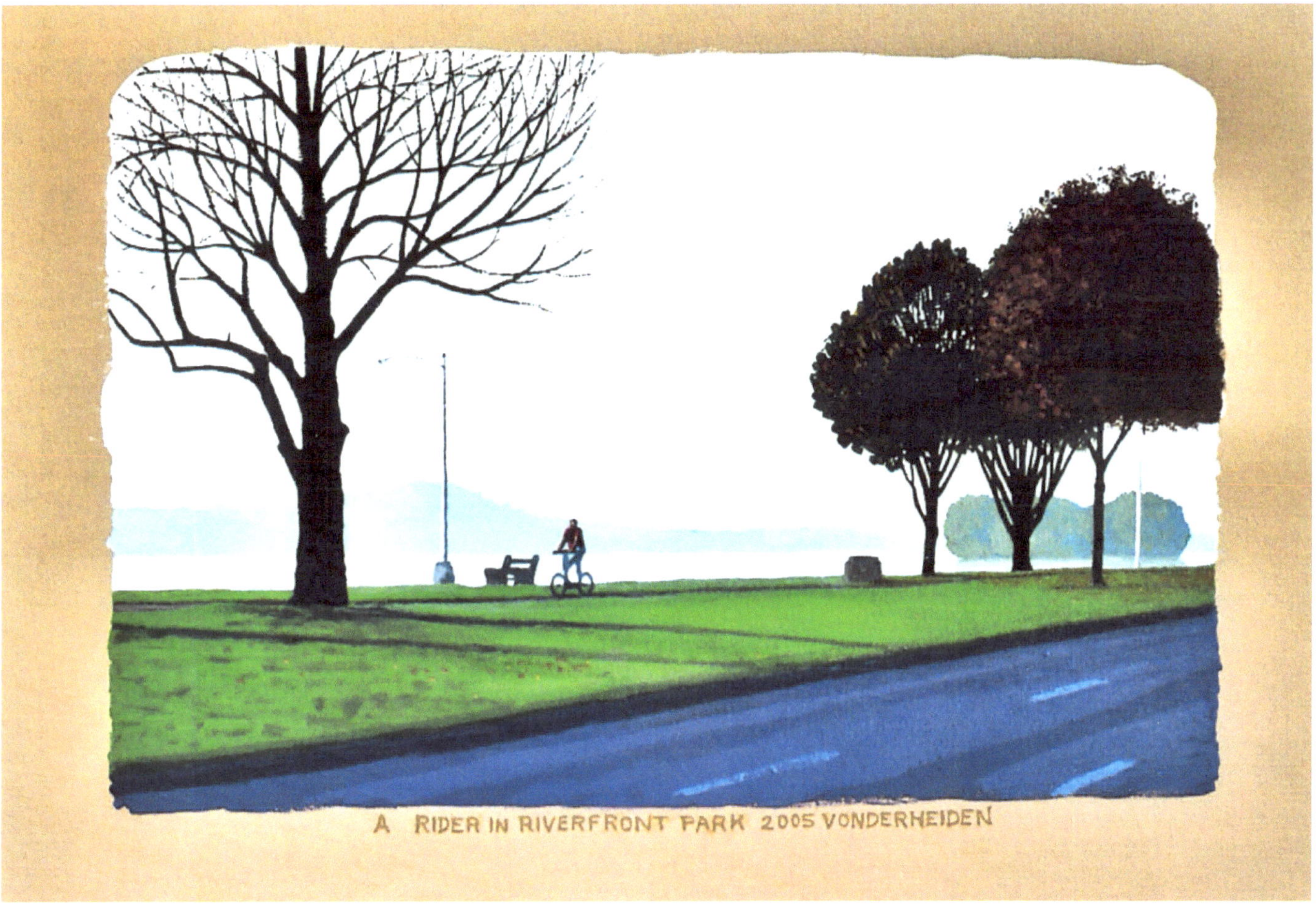

A Rider in Riverfront Park, 2005

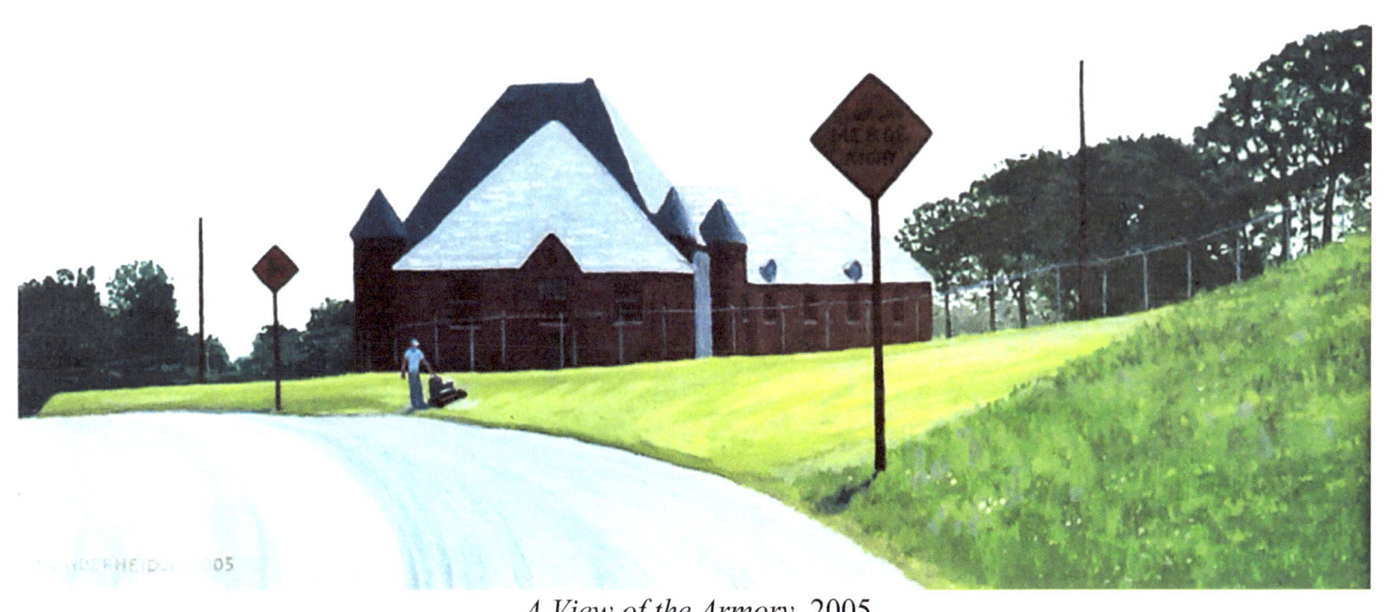

A View of the Armory, 2005

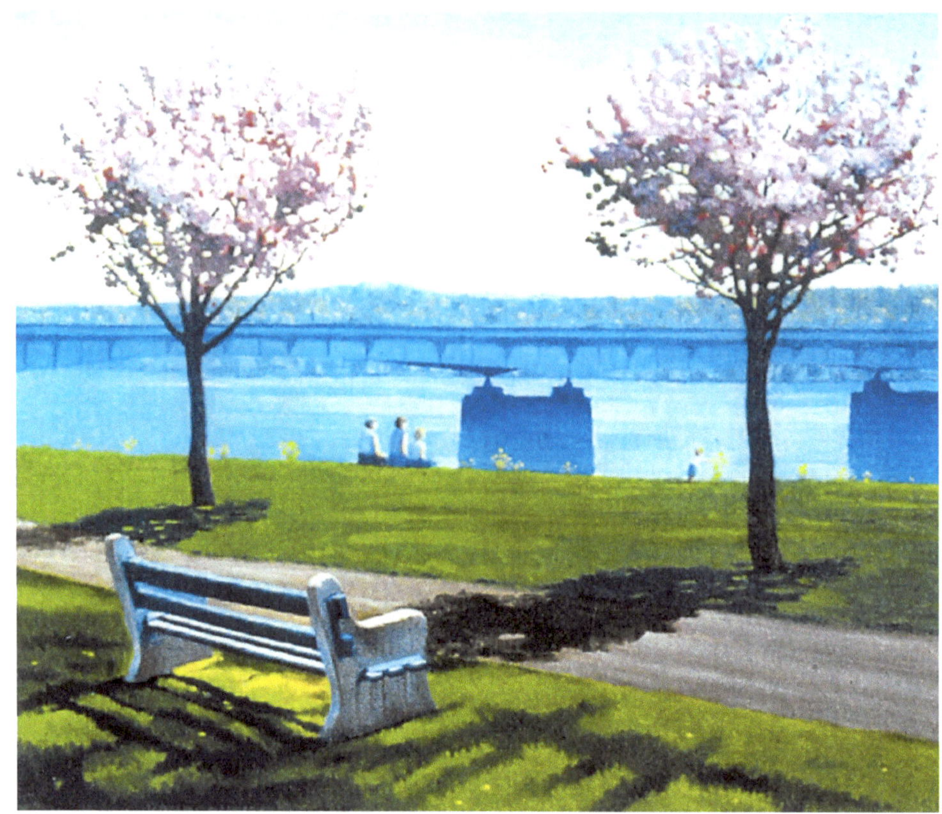

Blossoms and Bridge Piers, 2003

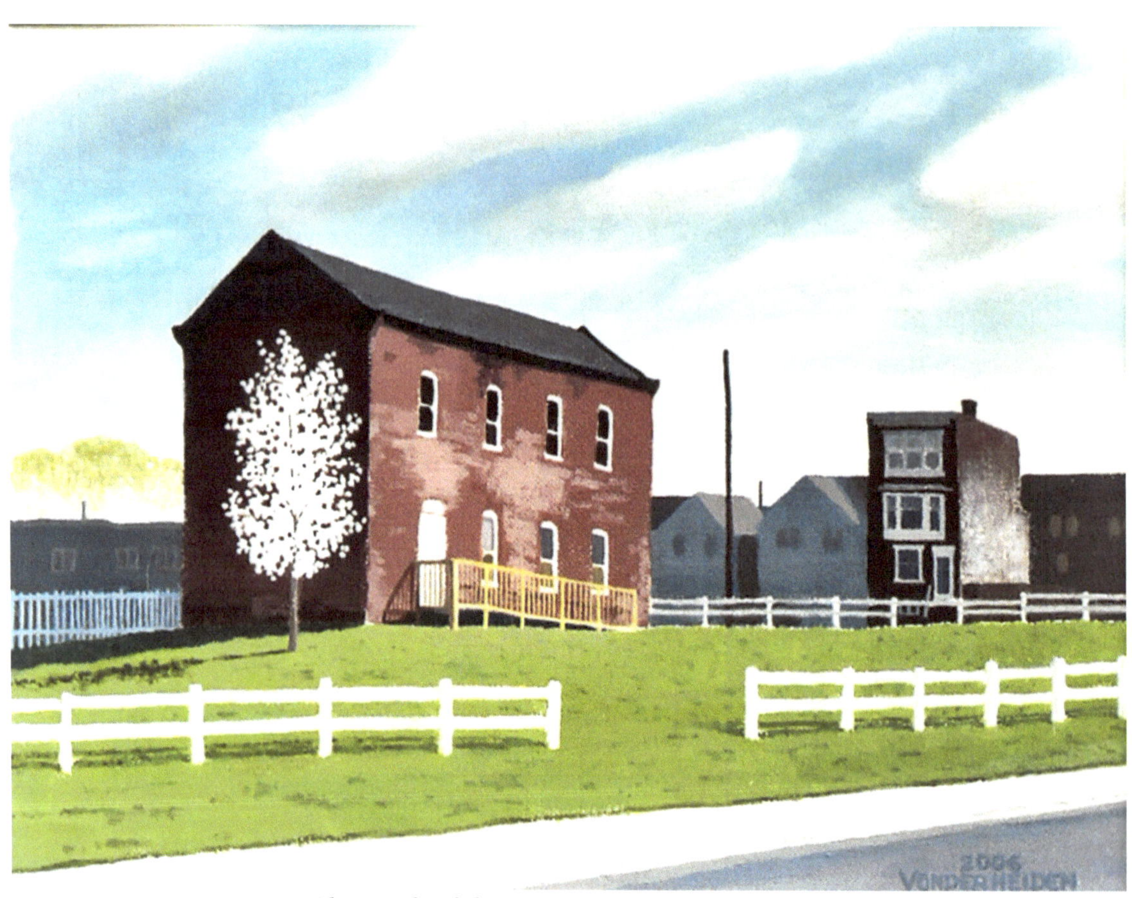

The Back of the Front Door Church, 2006

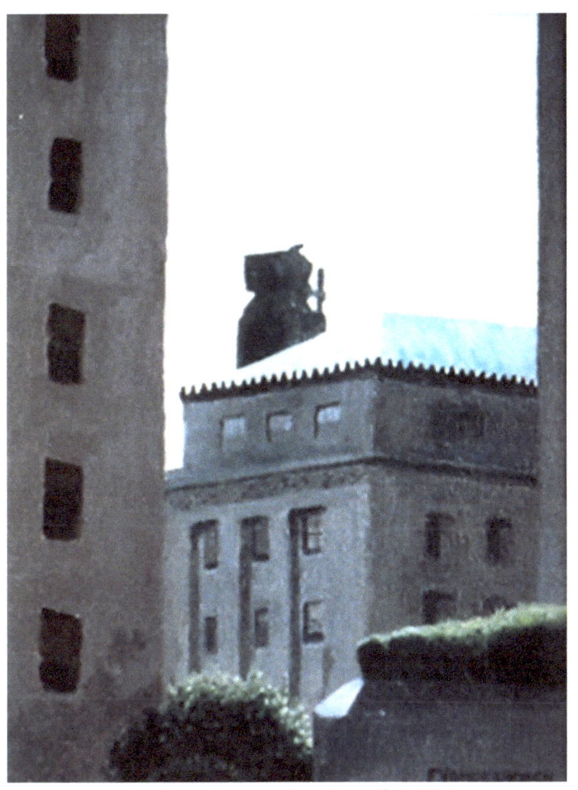

An Eagle on the Roof, 1995

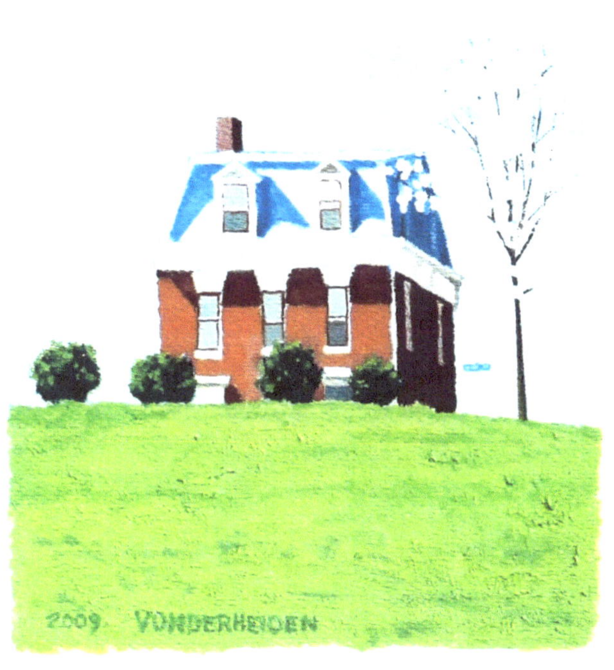

A House on North Sixth Street, 2010

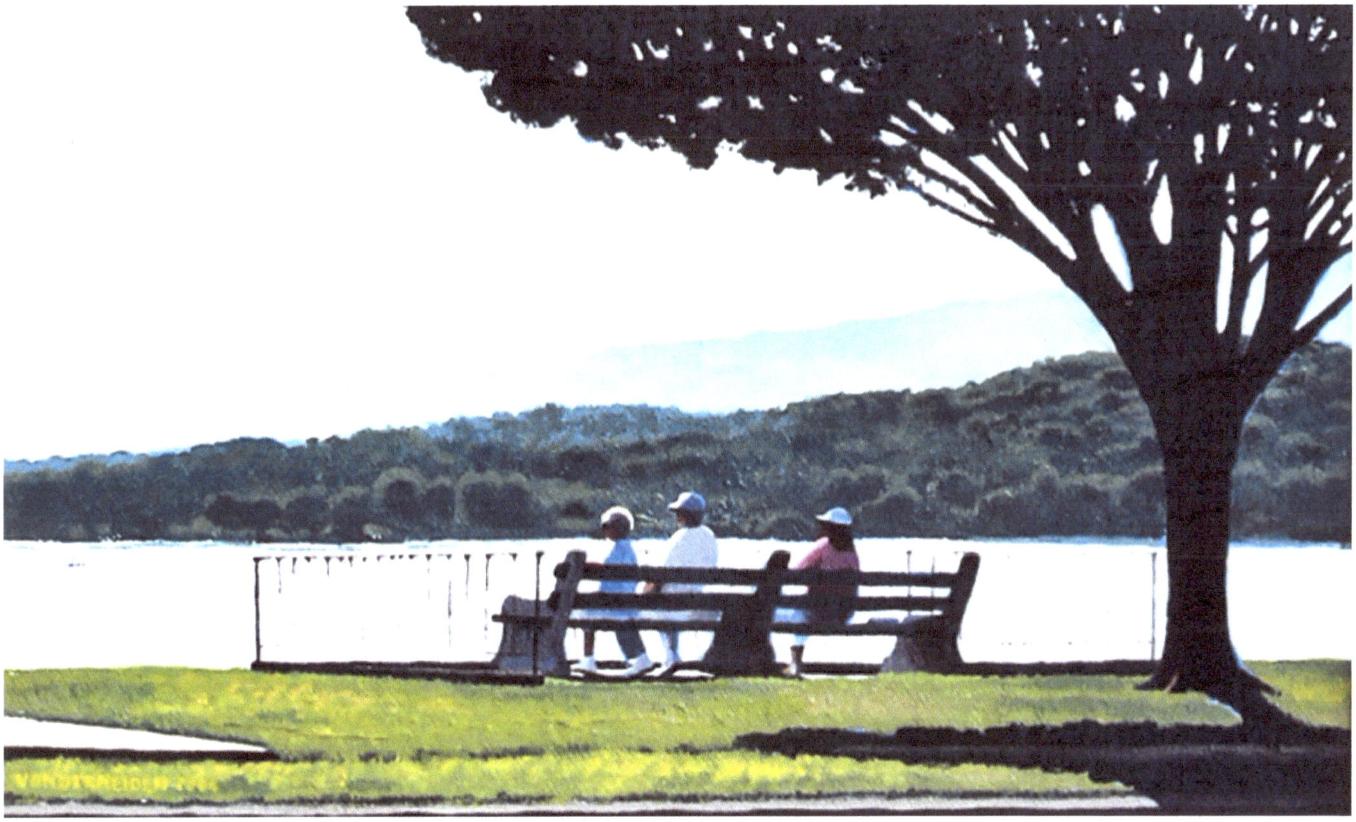

Parkbench People, 2004

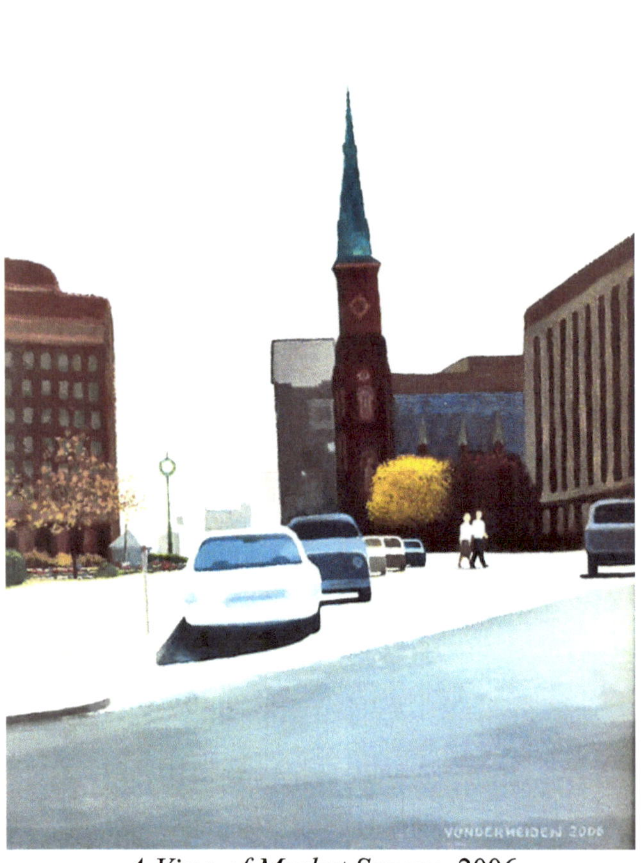

A View of Market Square, 2006

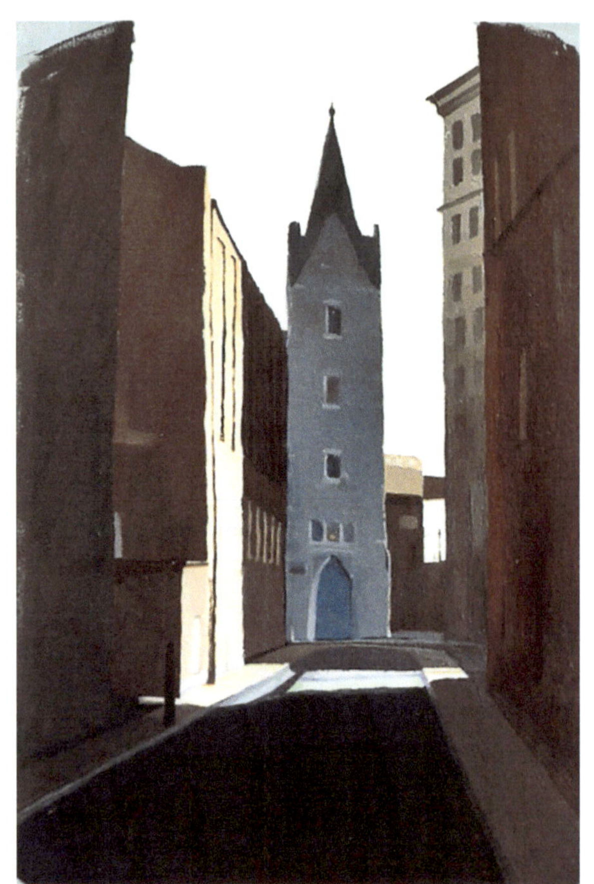

South on Susquehanna Street, 1998

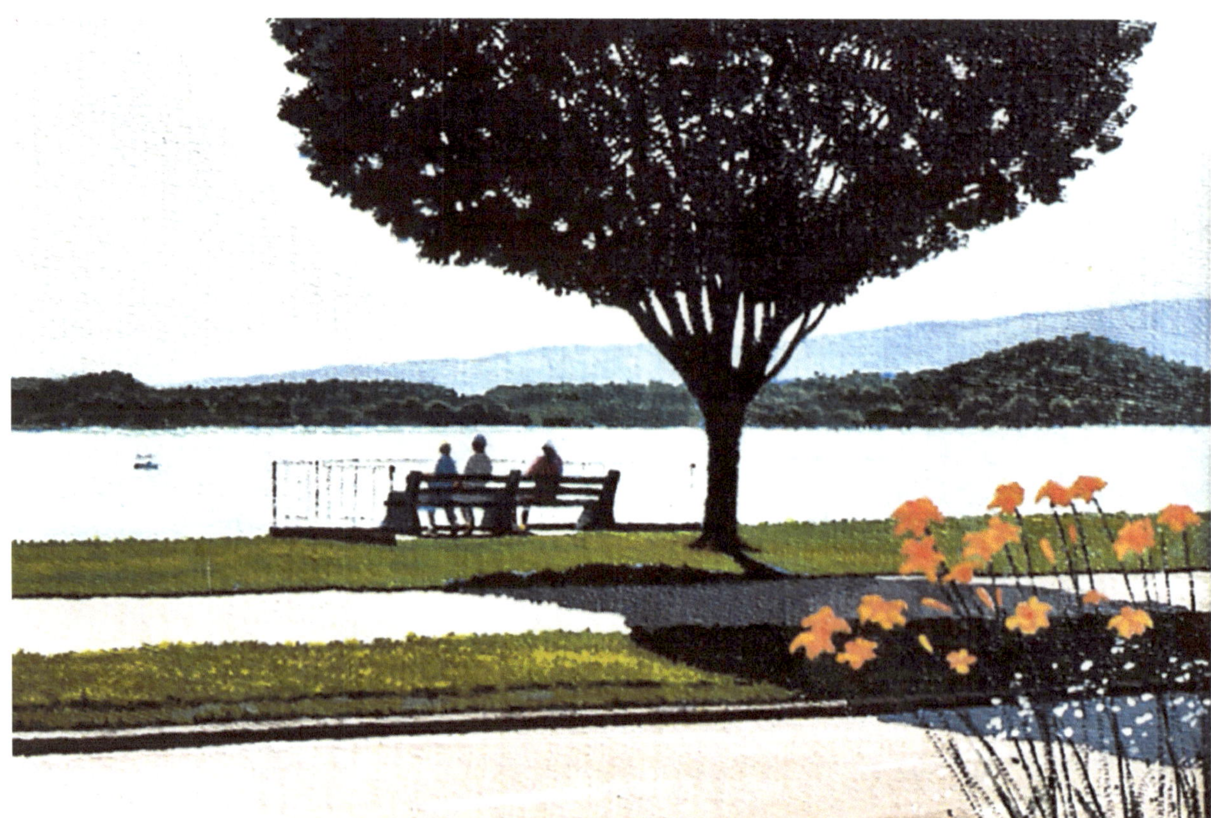

Parkbench People with Flowers, 2004

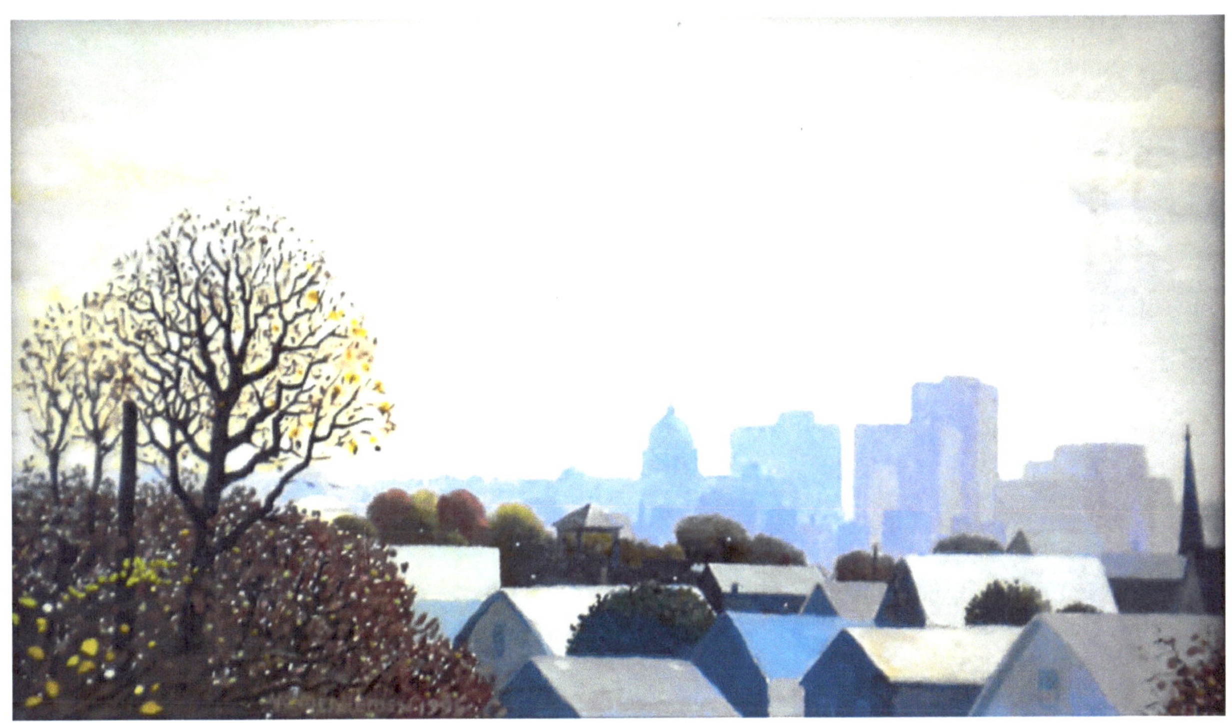

A View from Enola, 1995

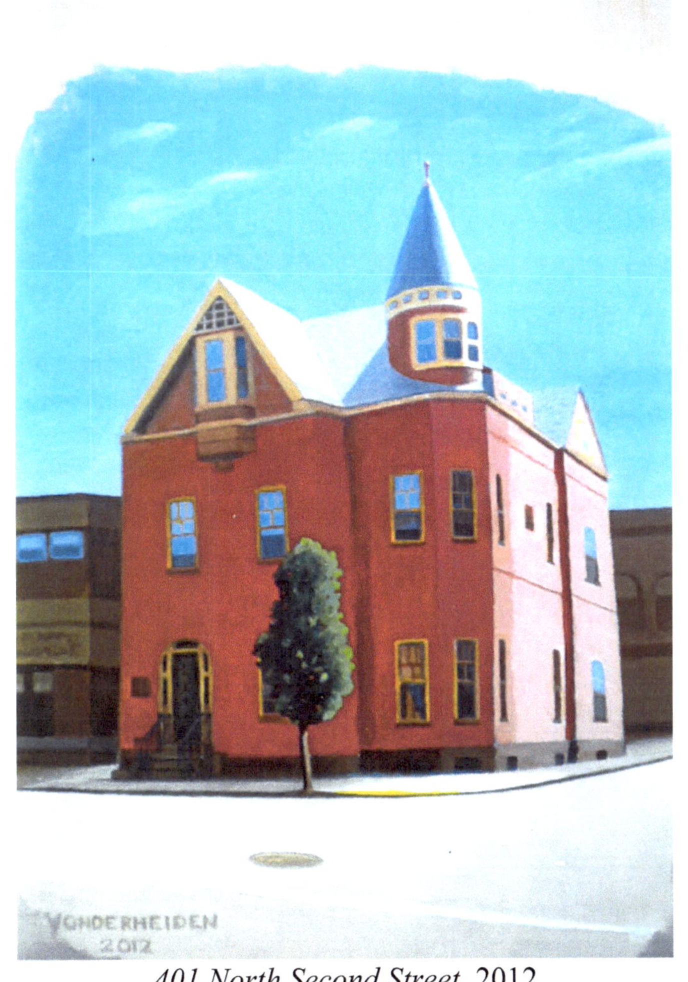

401 North Second Street, 2012

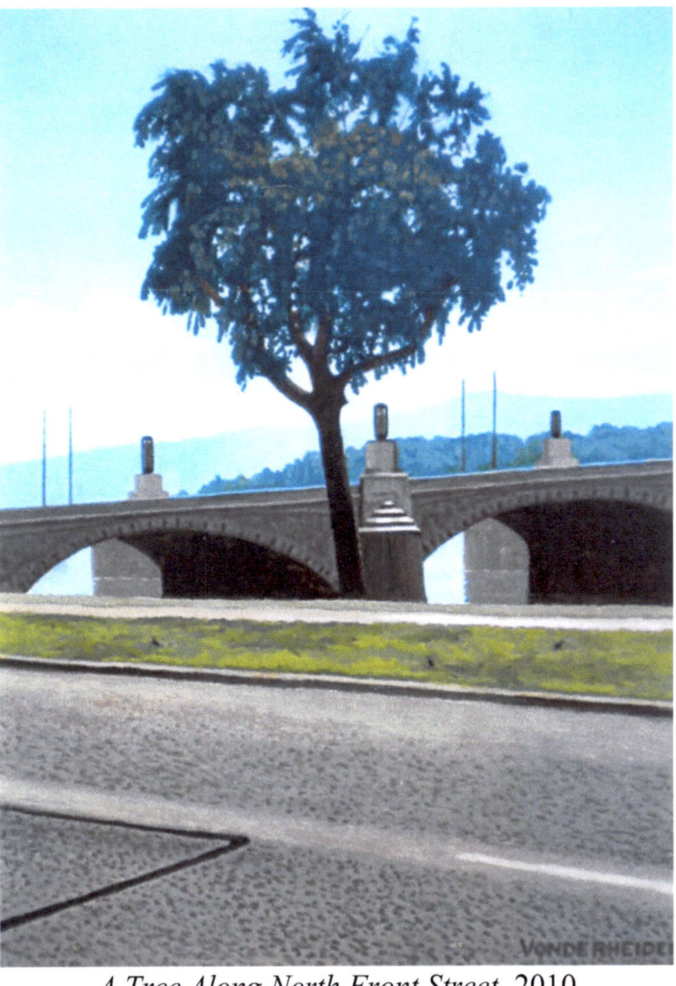

A Tree Along North Front Street, 2010

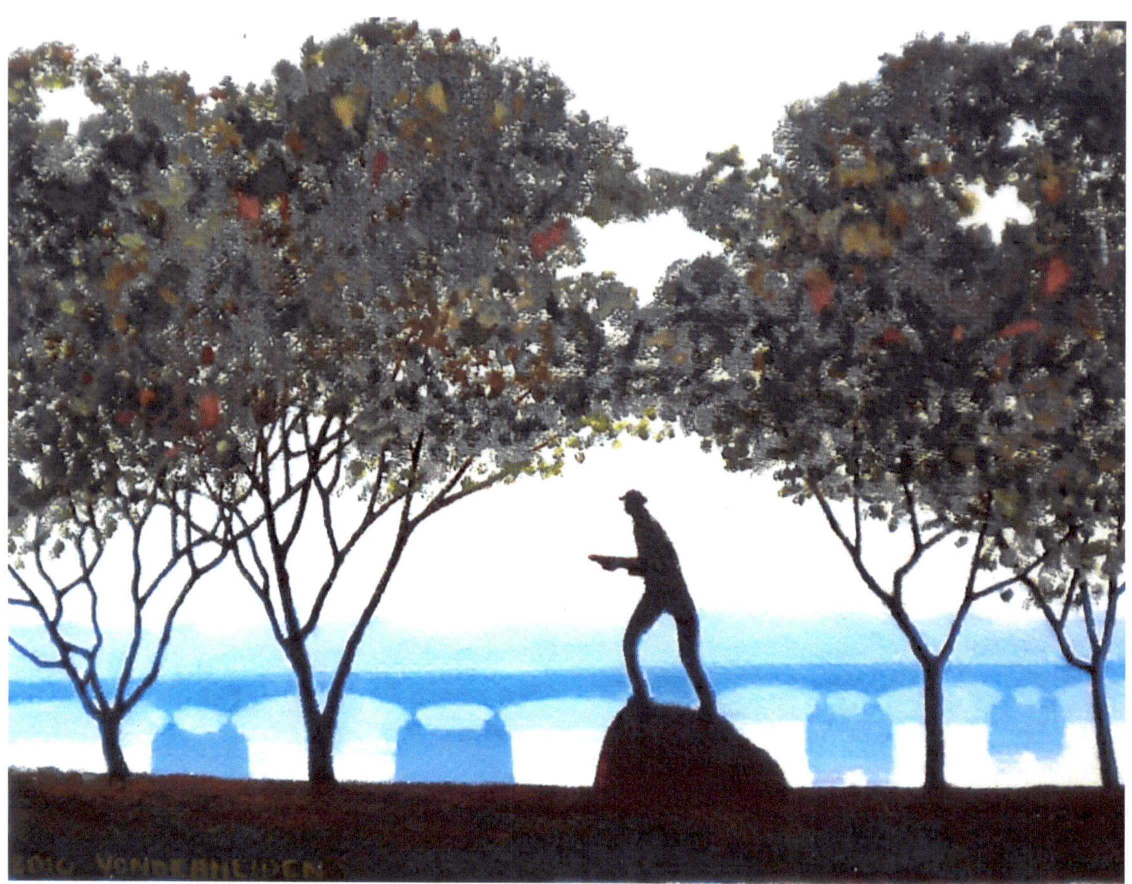

The Soldier in Riverfront Park, 2010

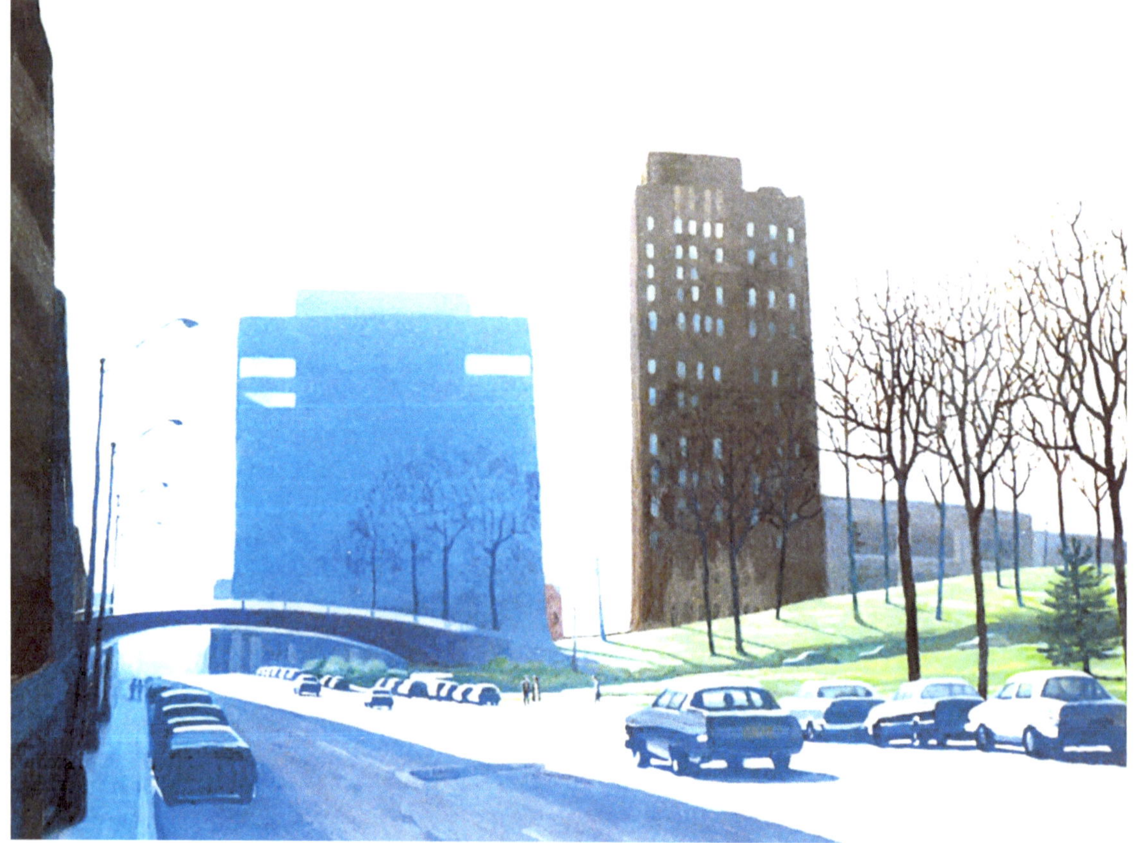

Sentinels of Capitol Park, 2000

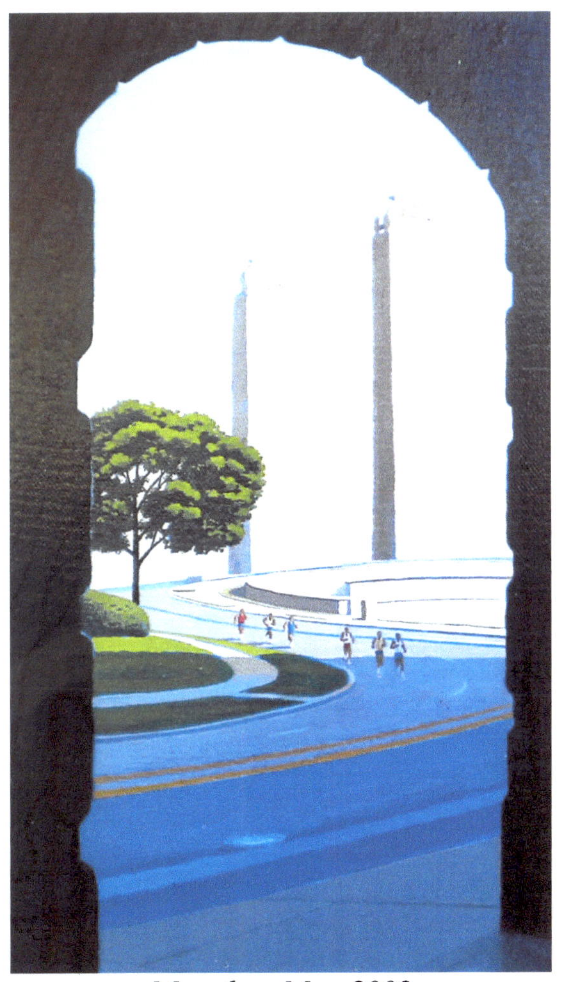
Marathon Men, 2003

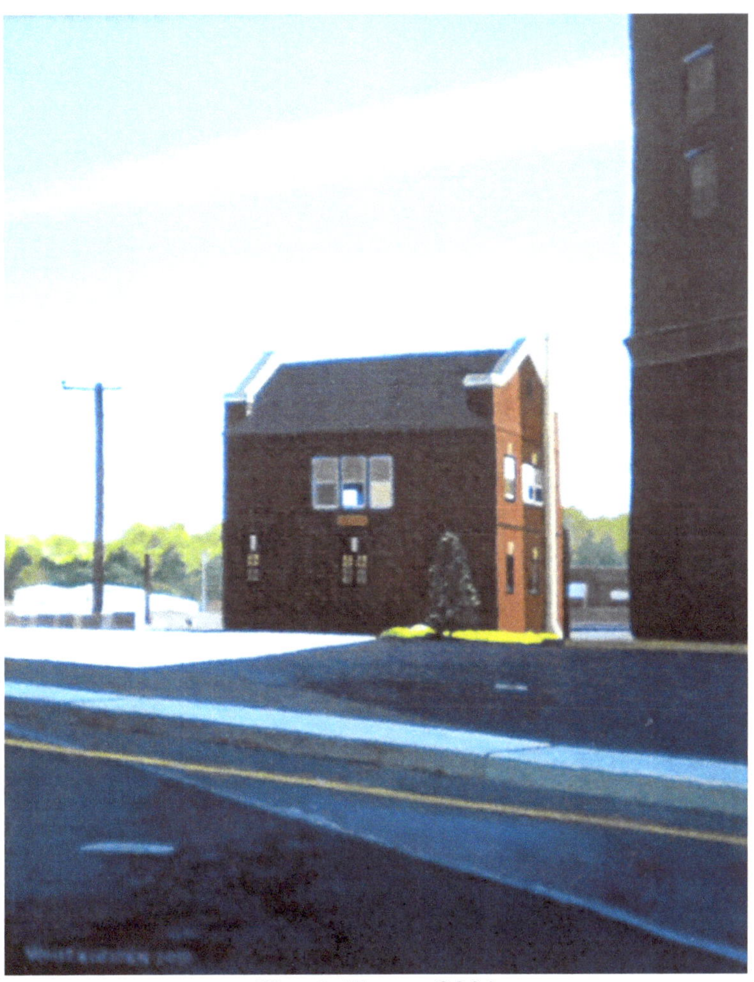
Harris Tower, 2001

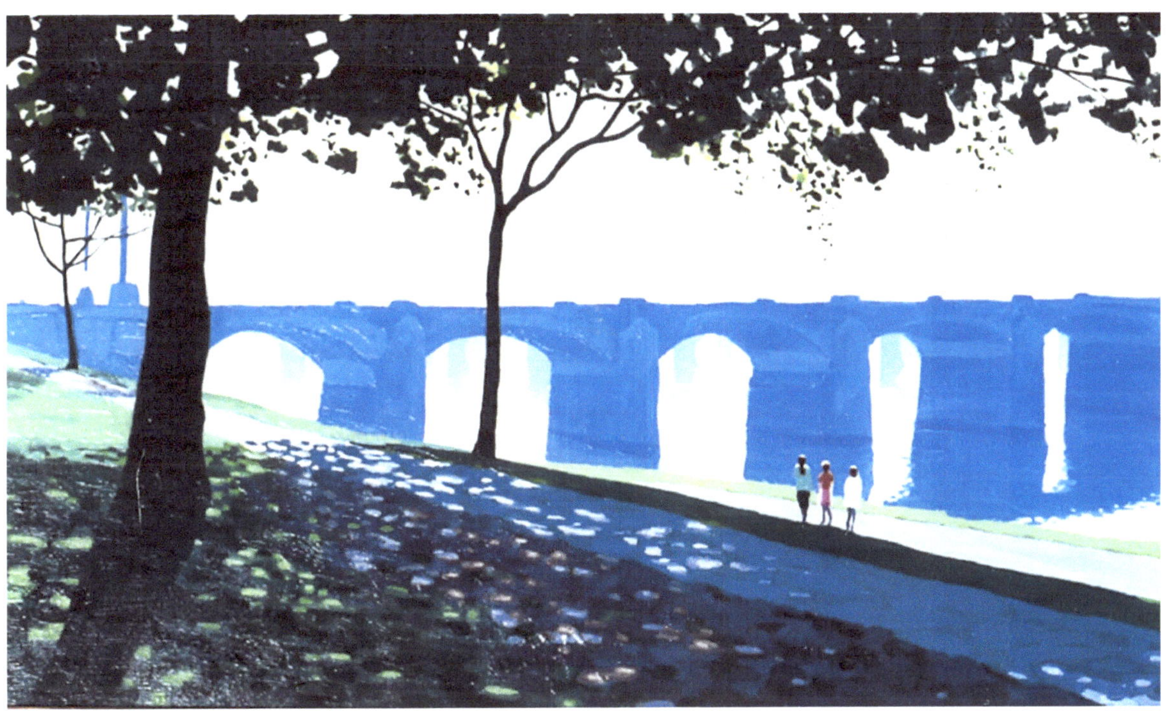
A View of the Market Street Bridge, 1997

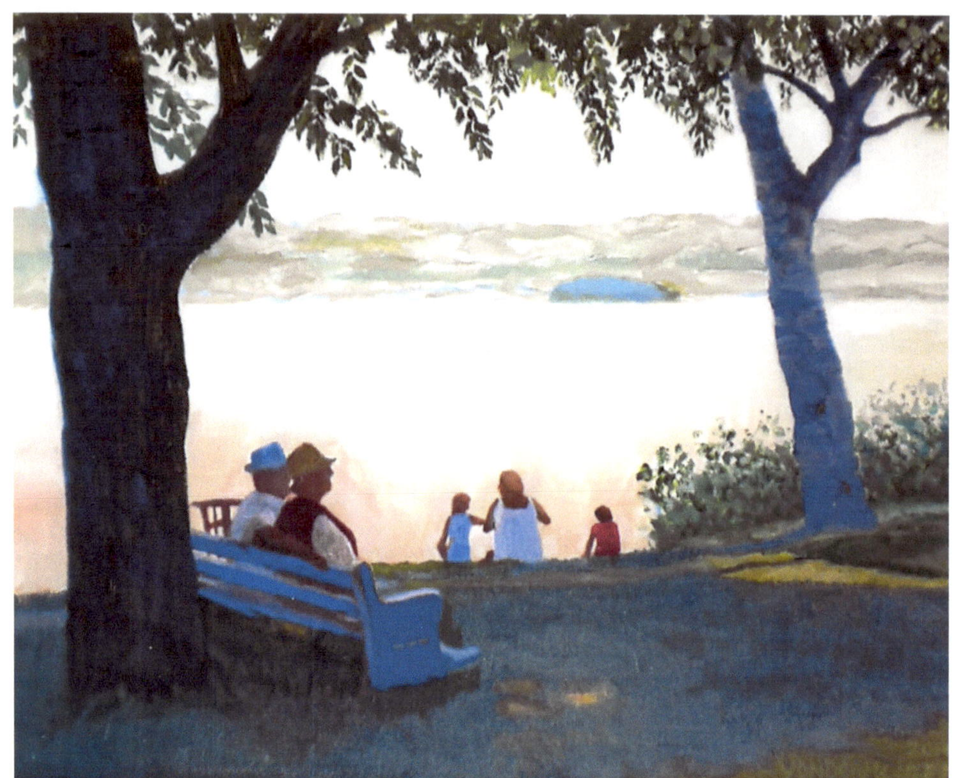

Relaxing by the River, 2014

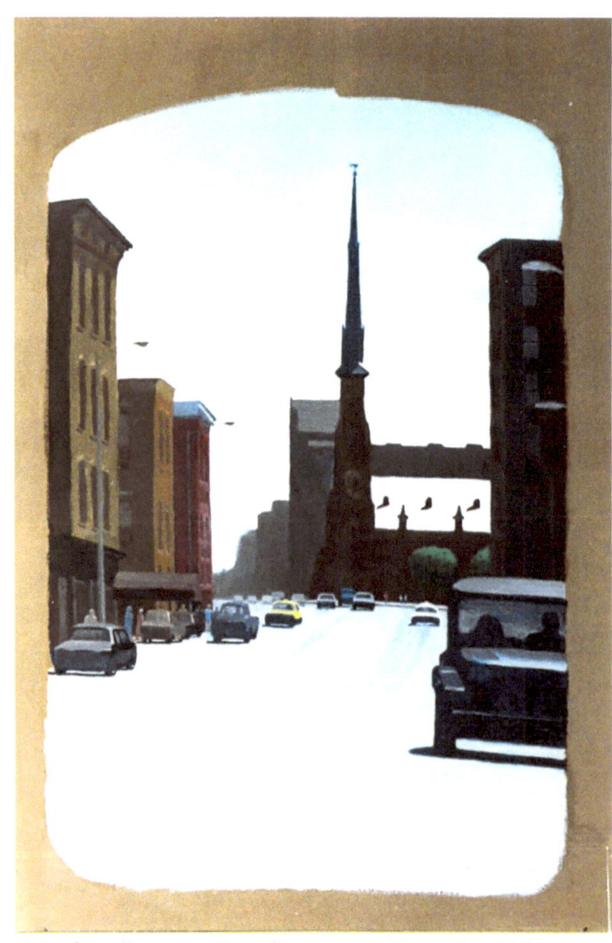

Market Square Presbyterian Church, 1993

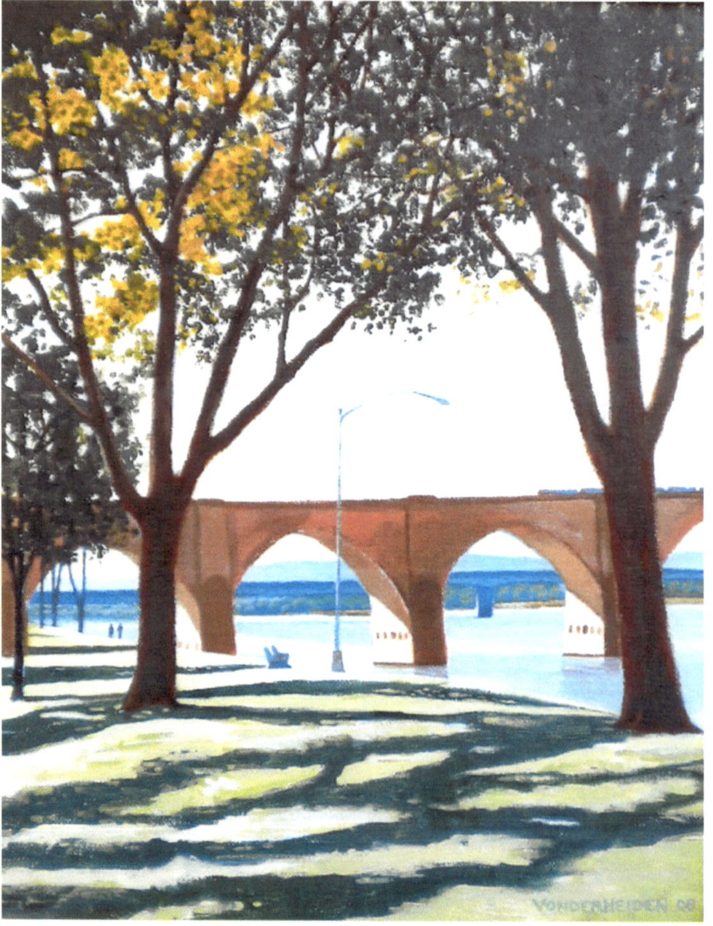

A View in Riverfront Park, 2008

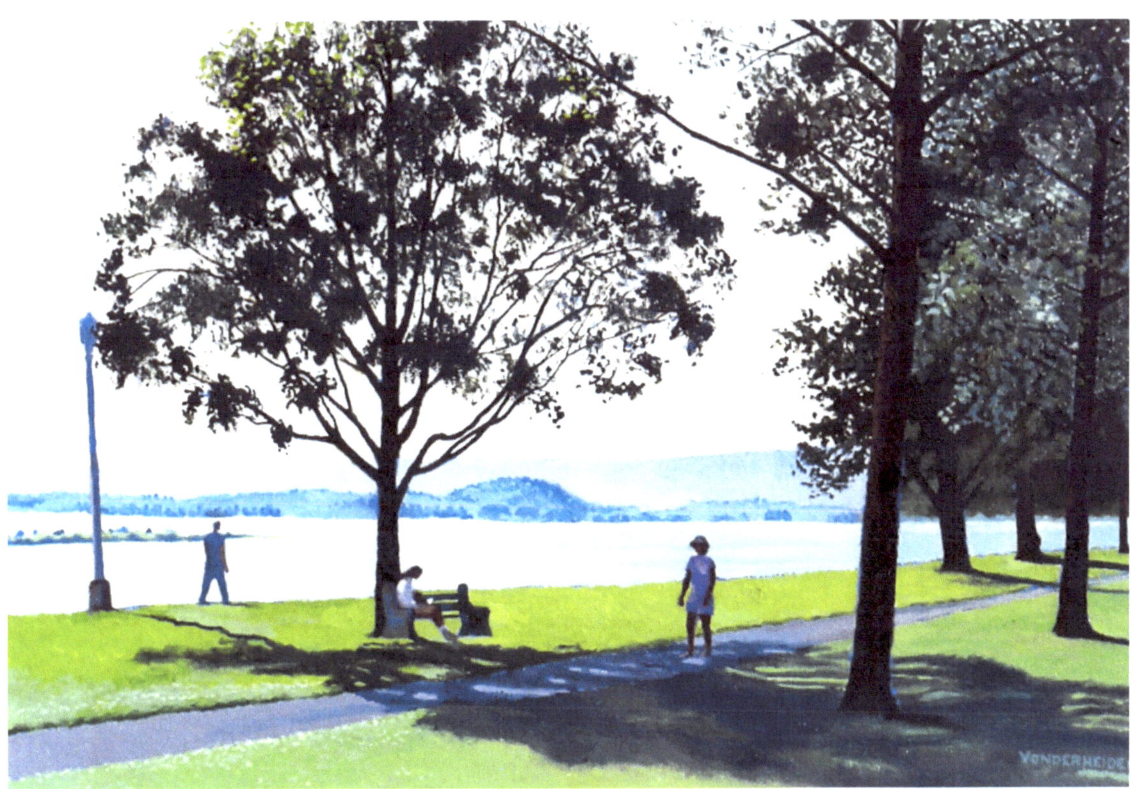

Strolling in Riverfront Park, 2006

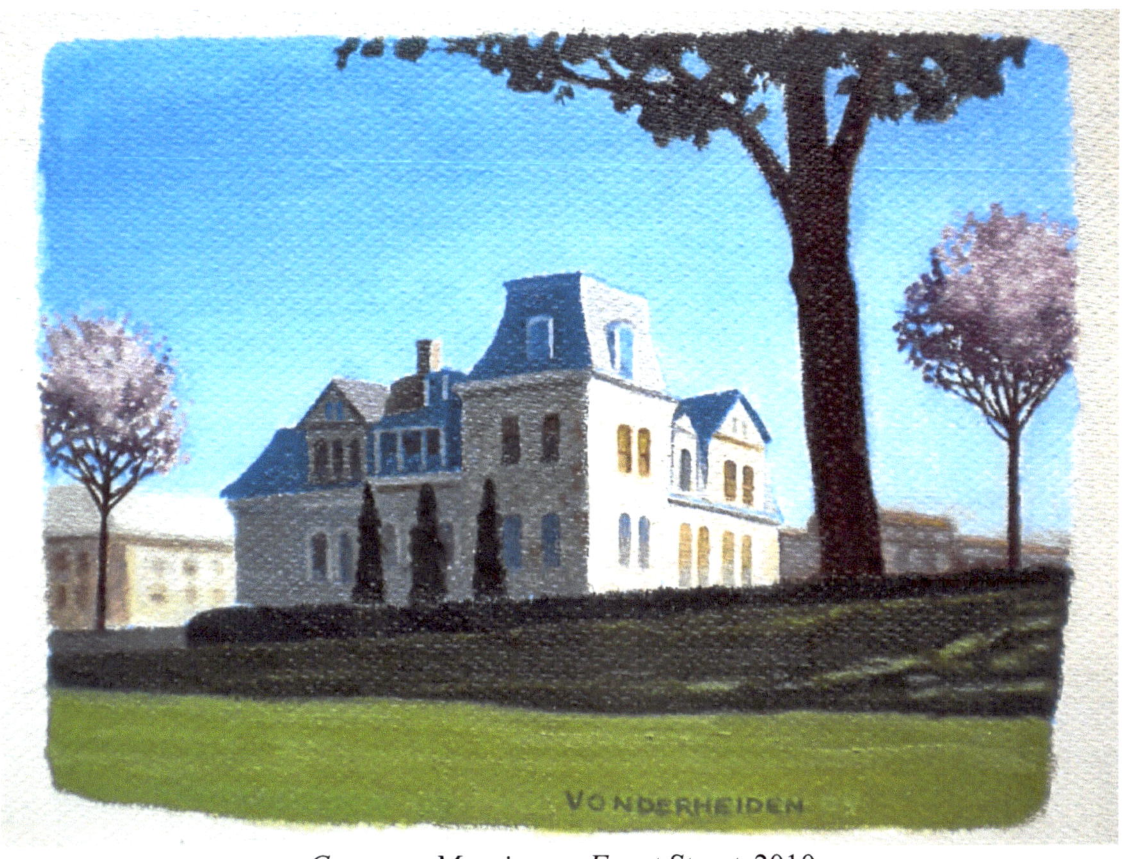

Cameron Mansion on Front Street, 2010

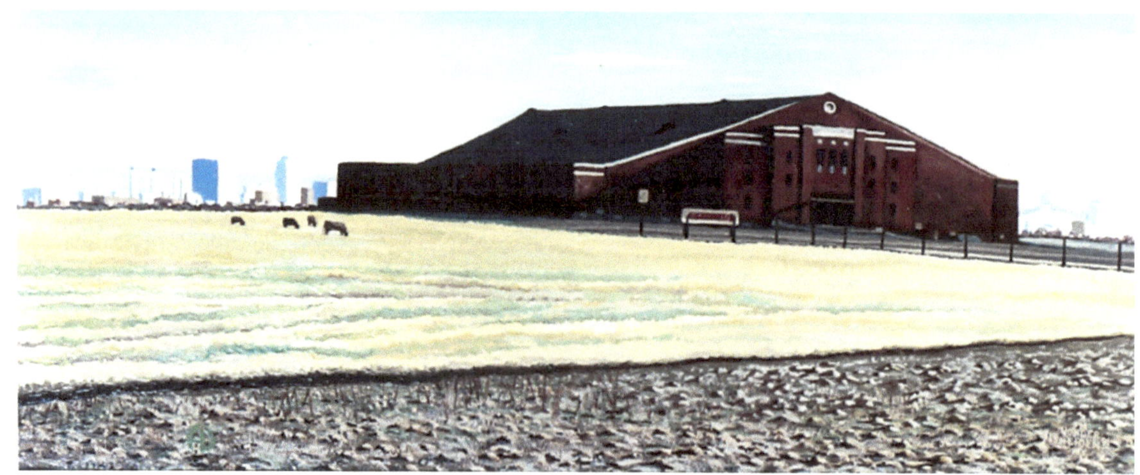

A View of the Farm Show Building, 1997

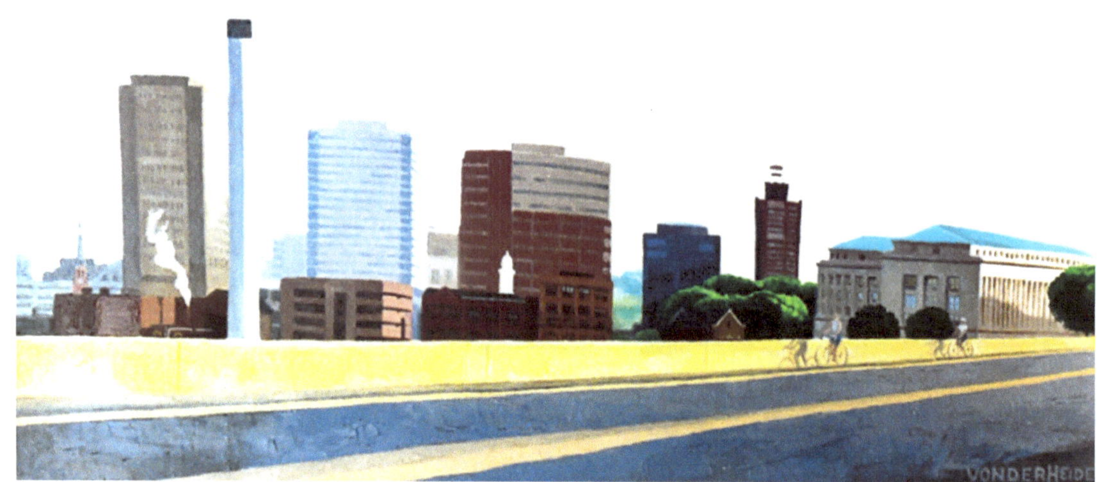

Keystone Skyline, 2005

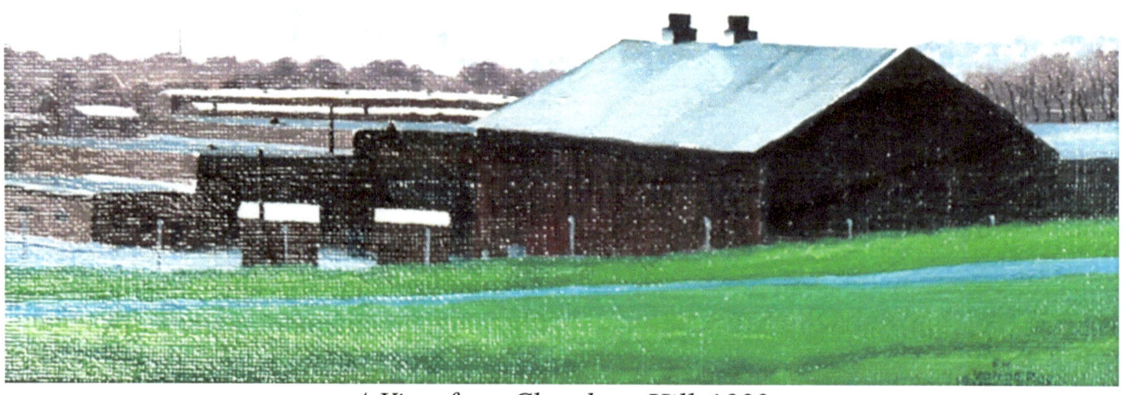

A View from Chambers Hill, 1999

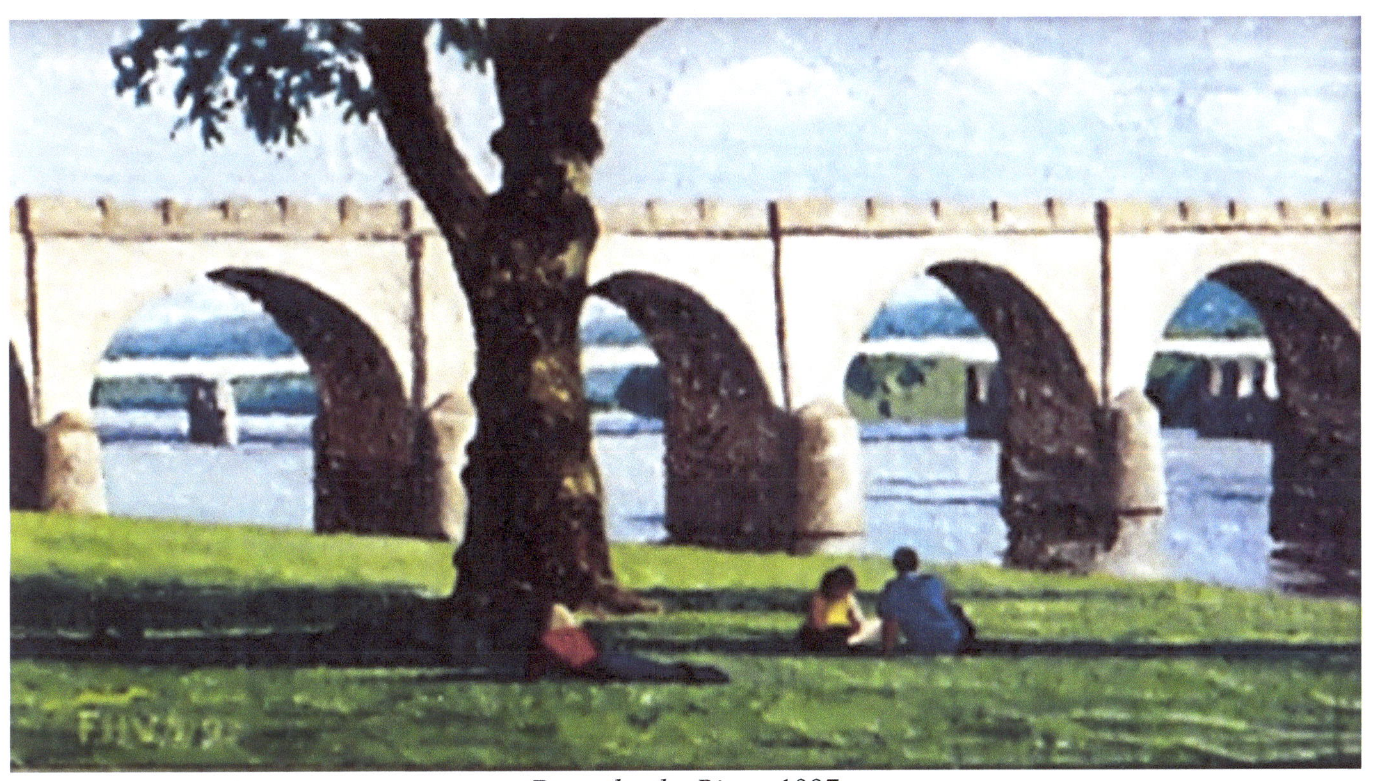

Down by the River, 1997

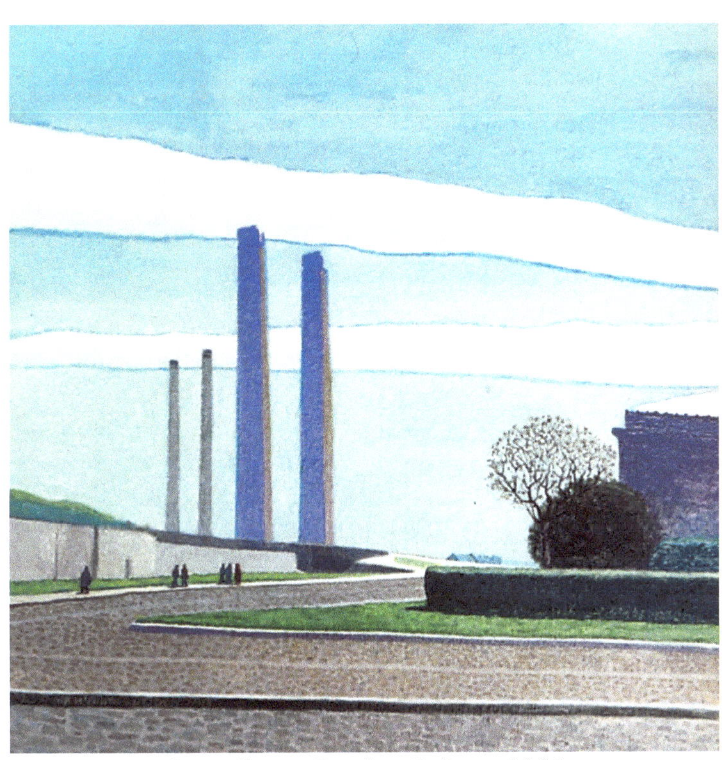

State Street Bridge Pylons, 1991

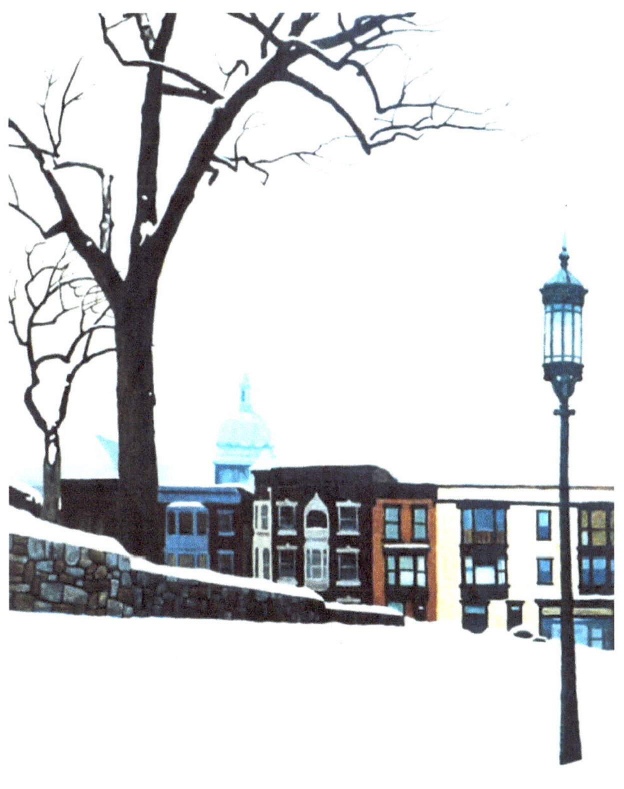

Third and North Streets, Winter, 1998

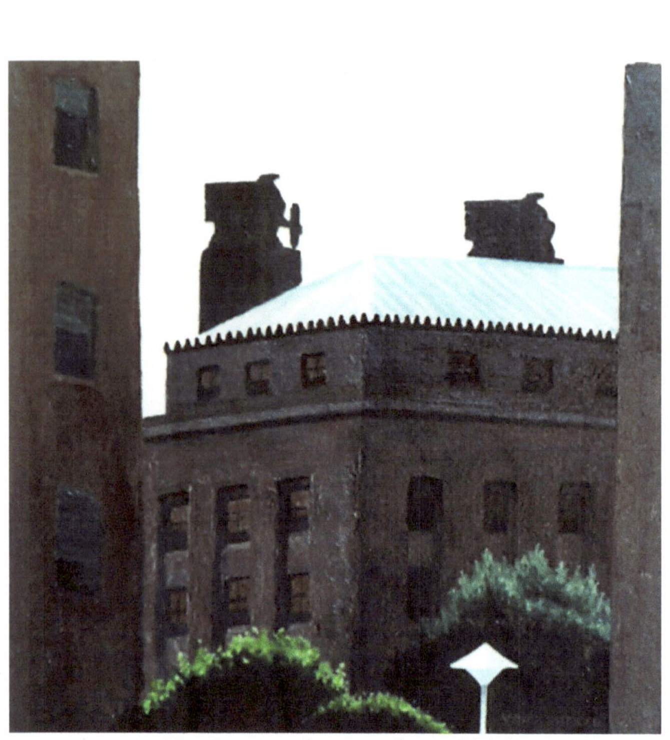

Eagles on the Rooftop, 1994

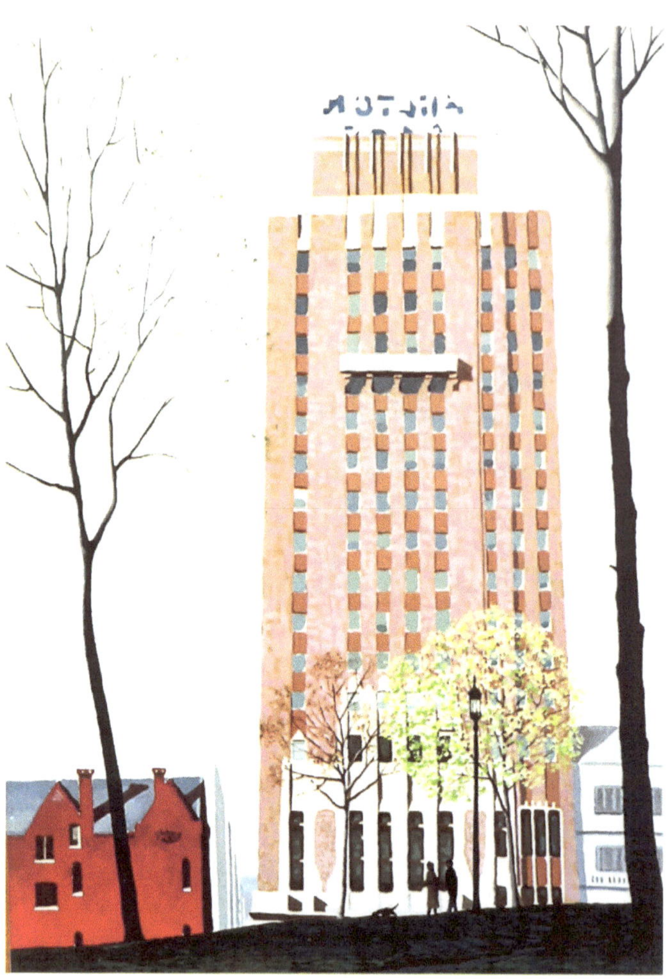

Fulton Bank Building, 1989

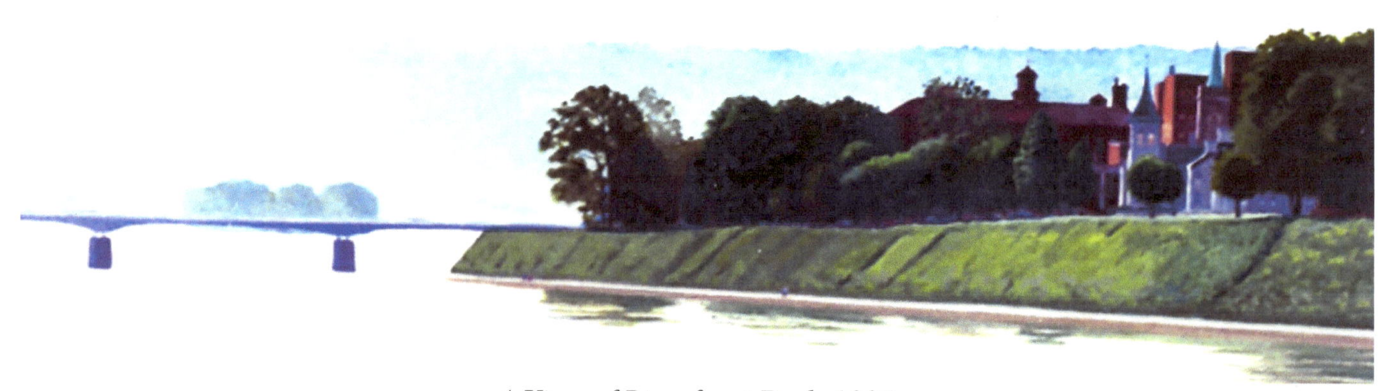

A View of Riverfront Park, 1995

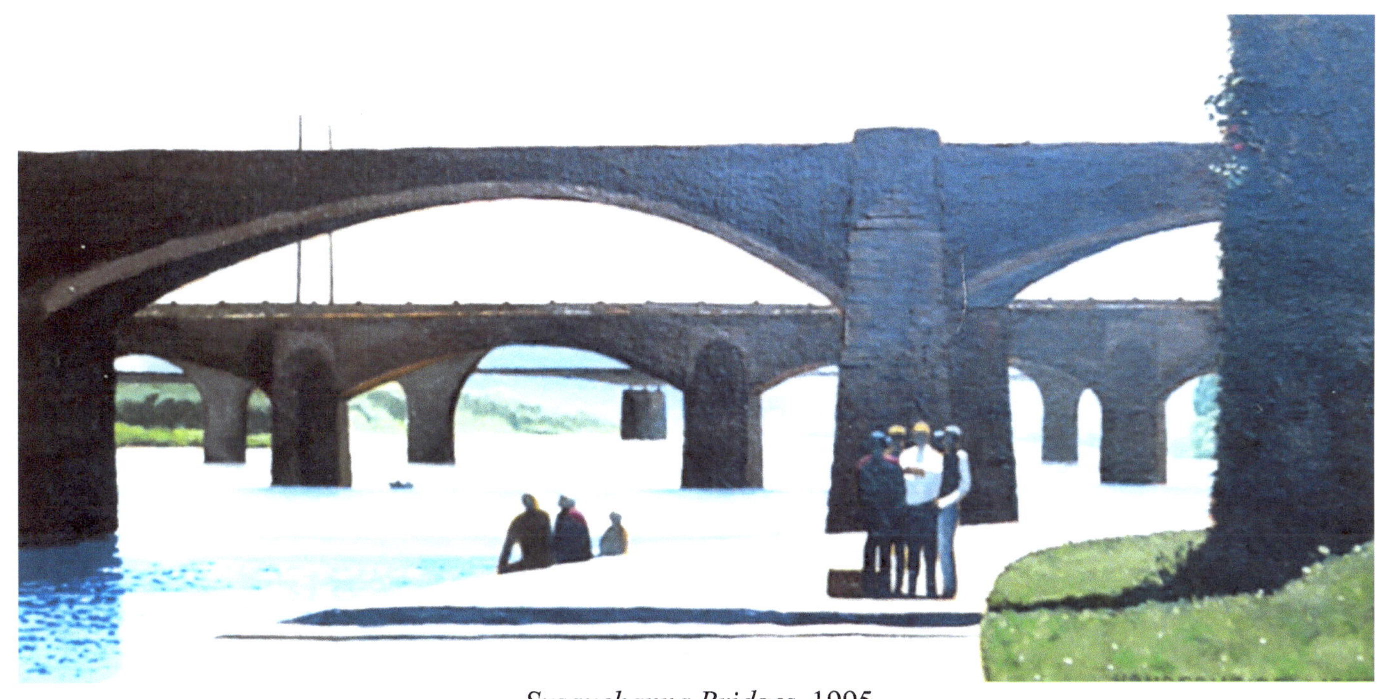

Susquehanna Bridges, 1995

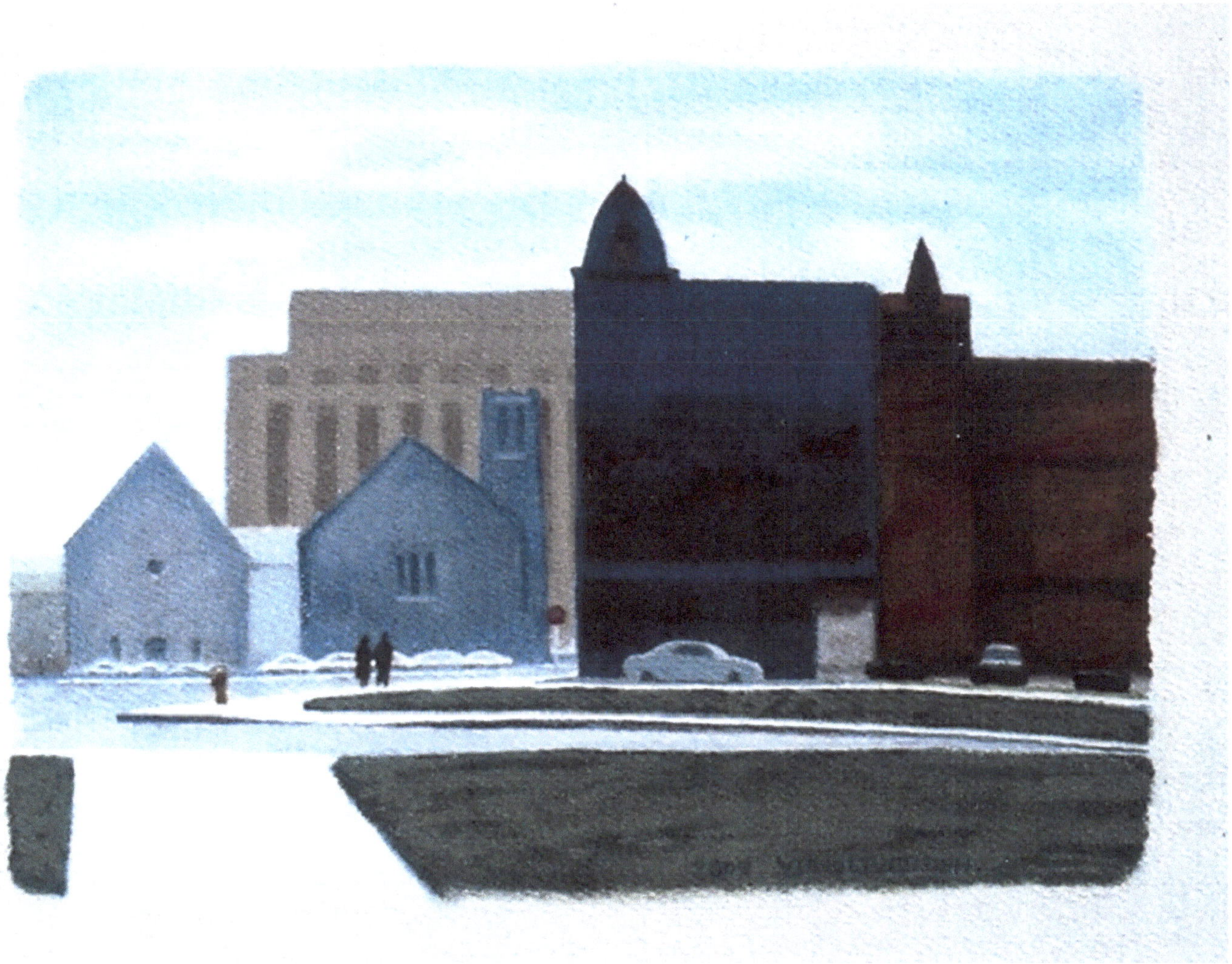

Shapes of the City, 2009

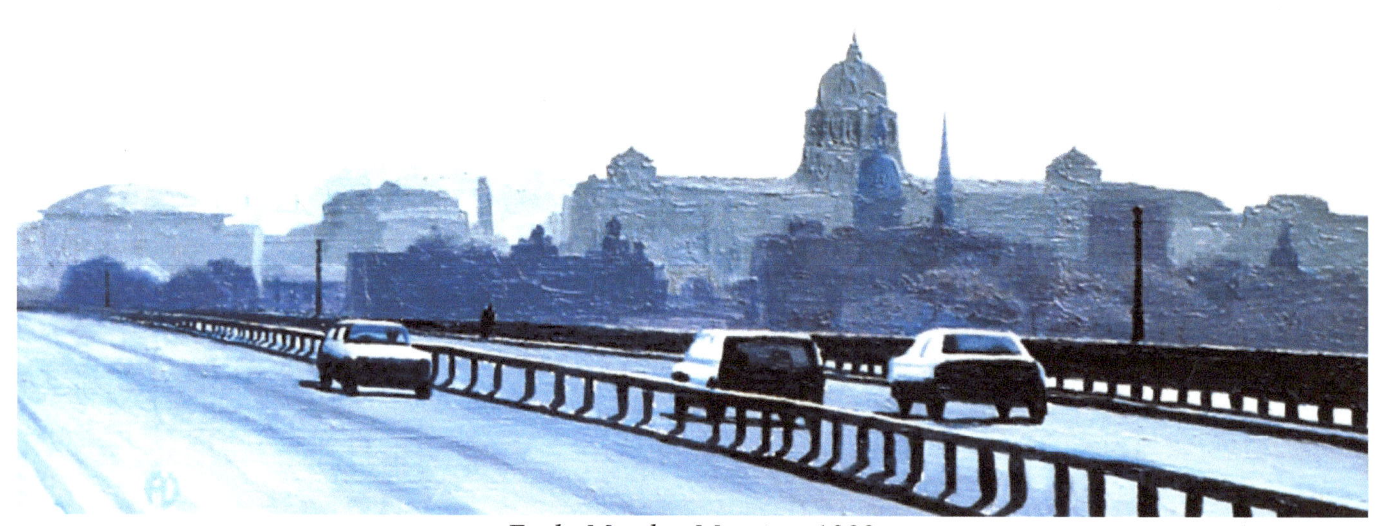

Early Monday Morning, 1992

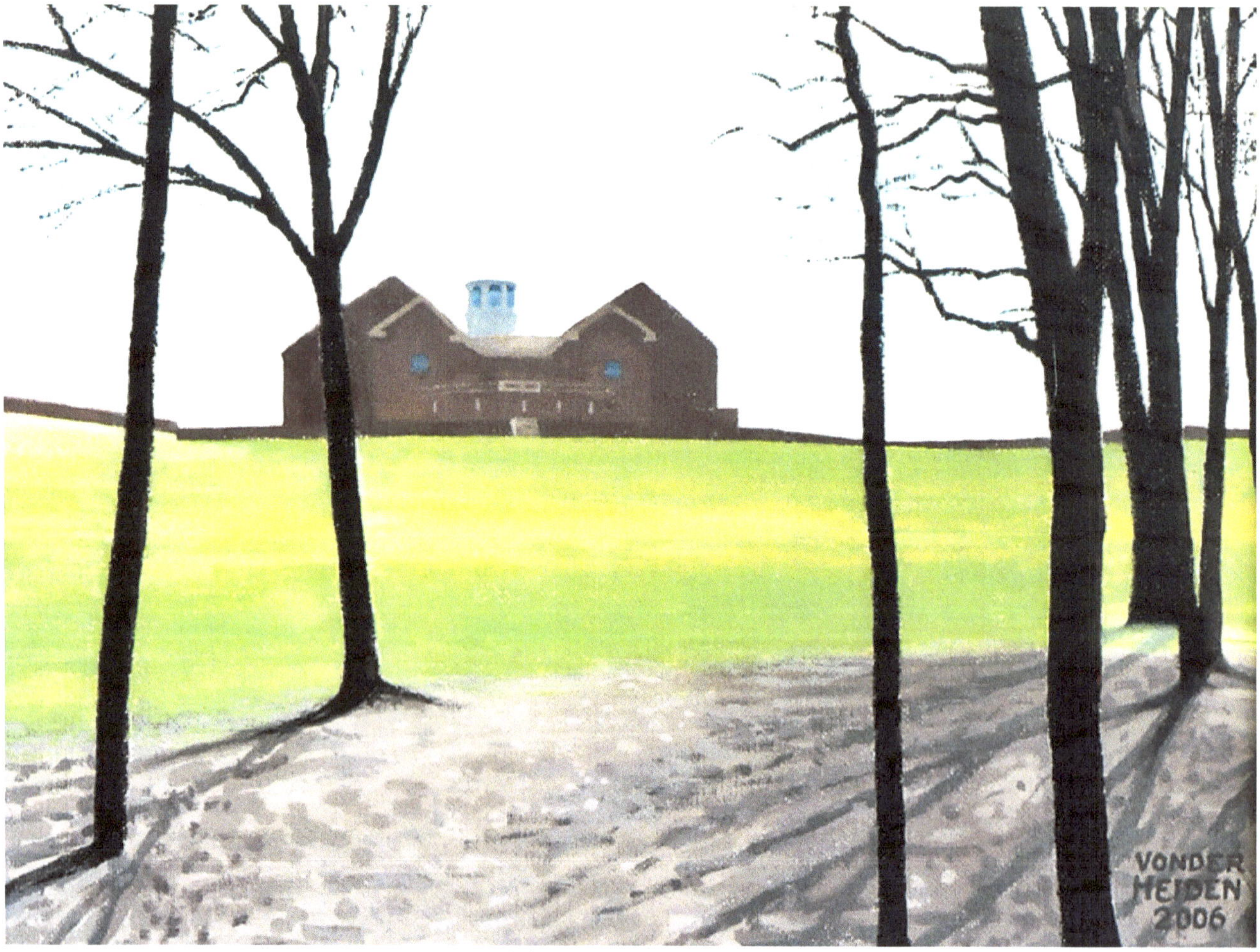

A View of the Civil War Museum, 2006

Scenes of the Greater Harrisburg Area

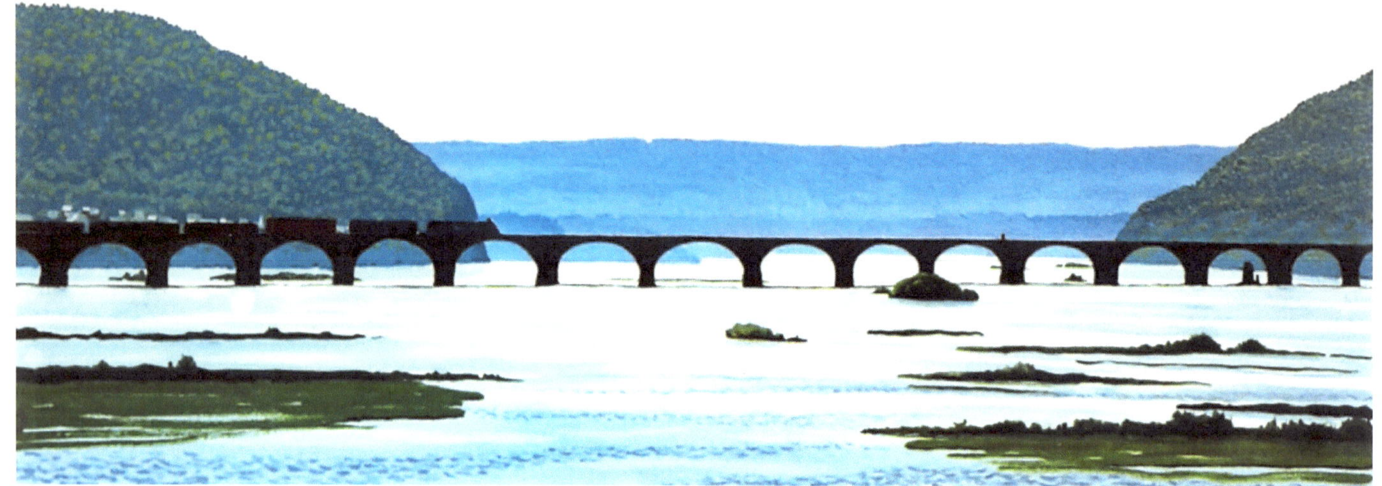

The Rockville Bridge, 1992

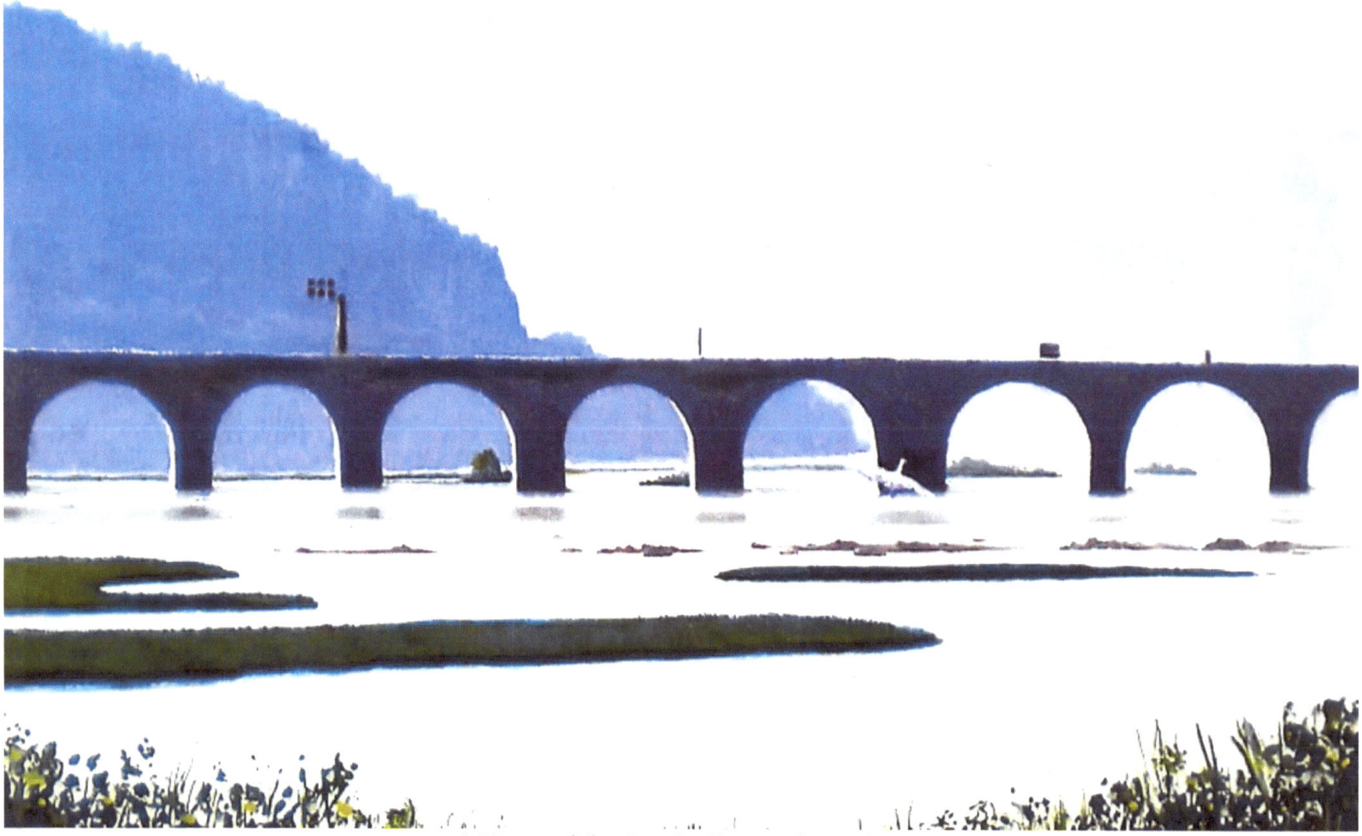

A View of the Rockville Bridge, 1997

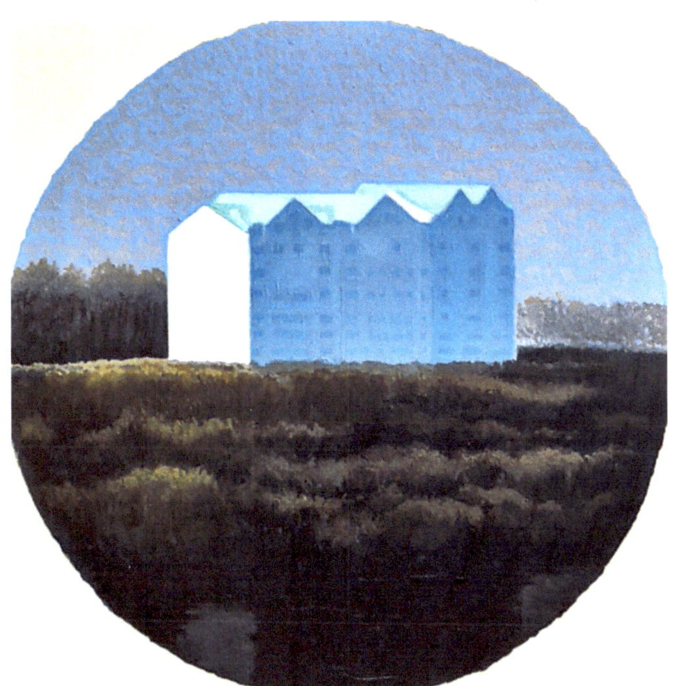

The Waterford, 1990

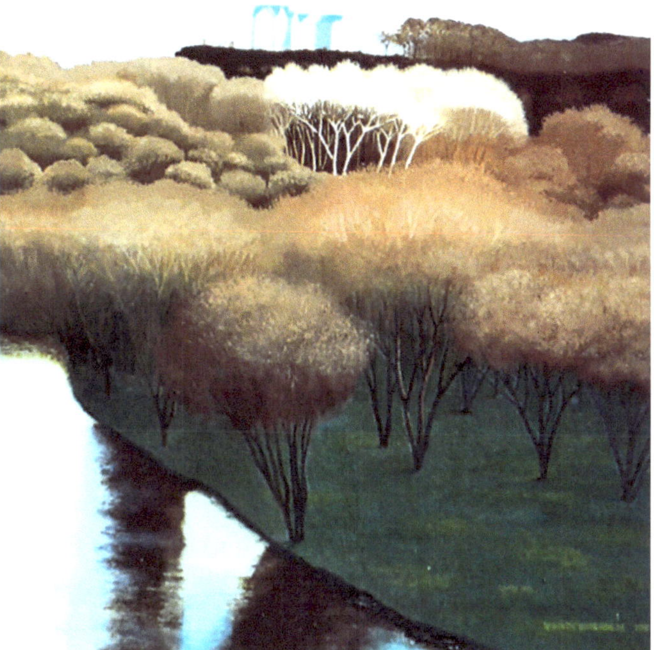

The Waterford in Winter, 1998

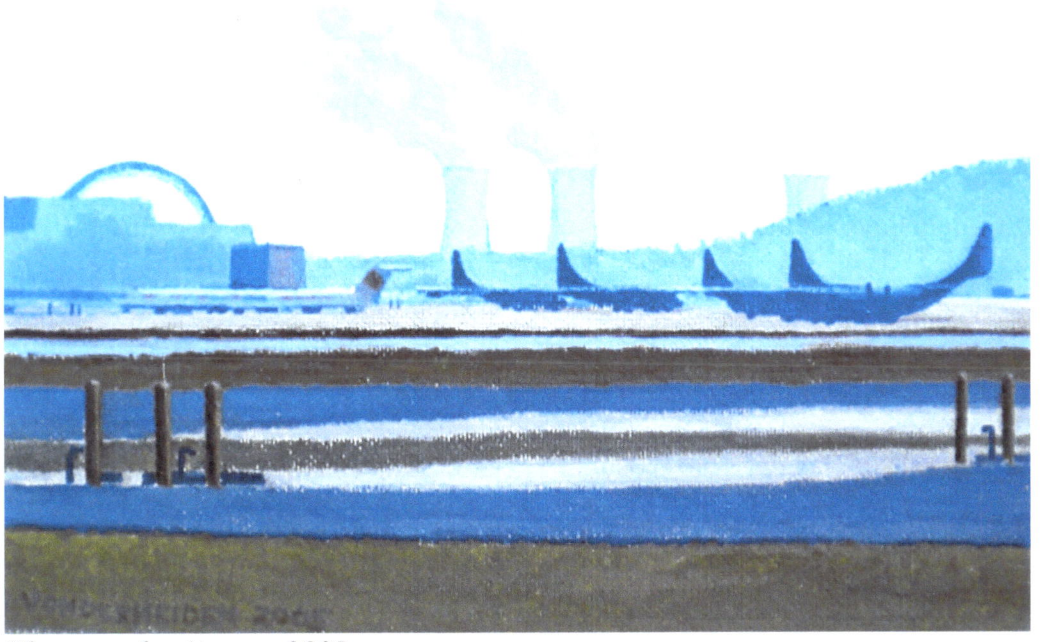

Planes at the Airport, 2005

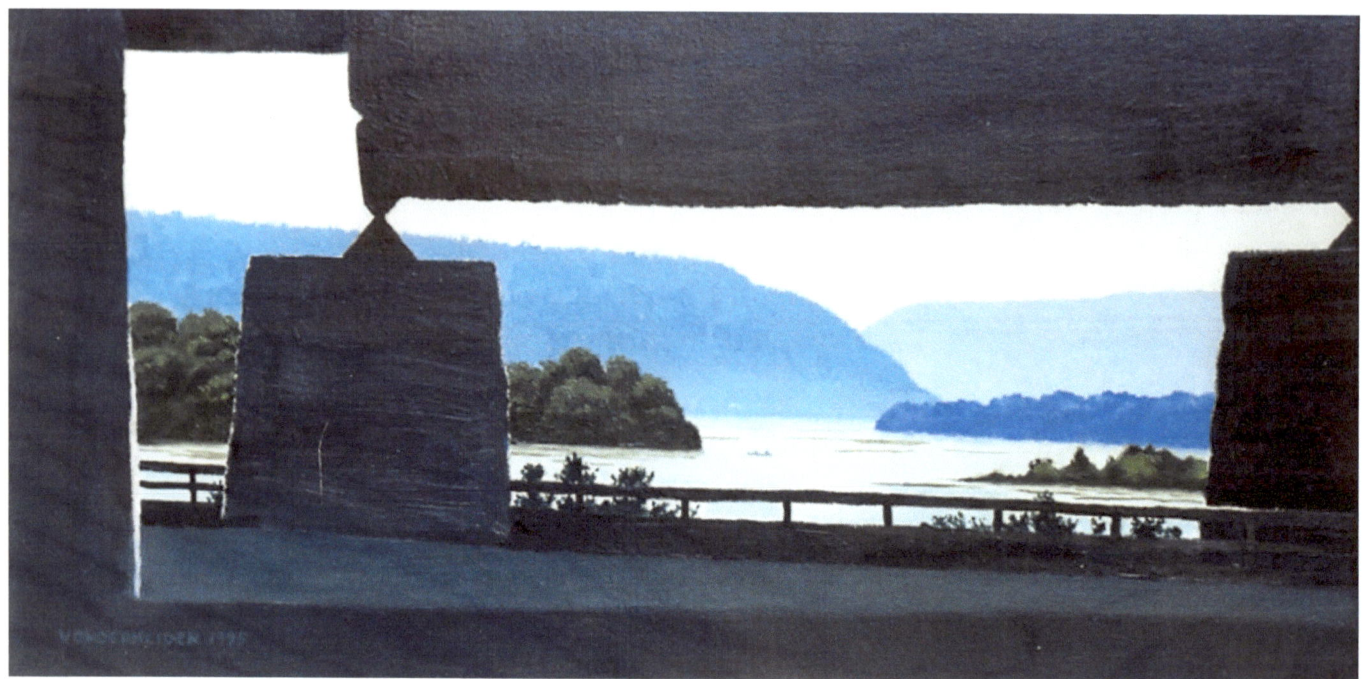

West Shore Bridge Piers, 1988

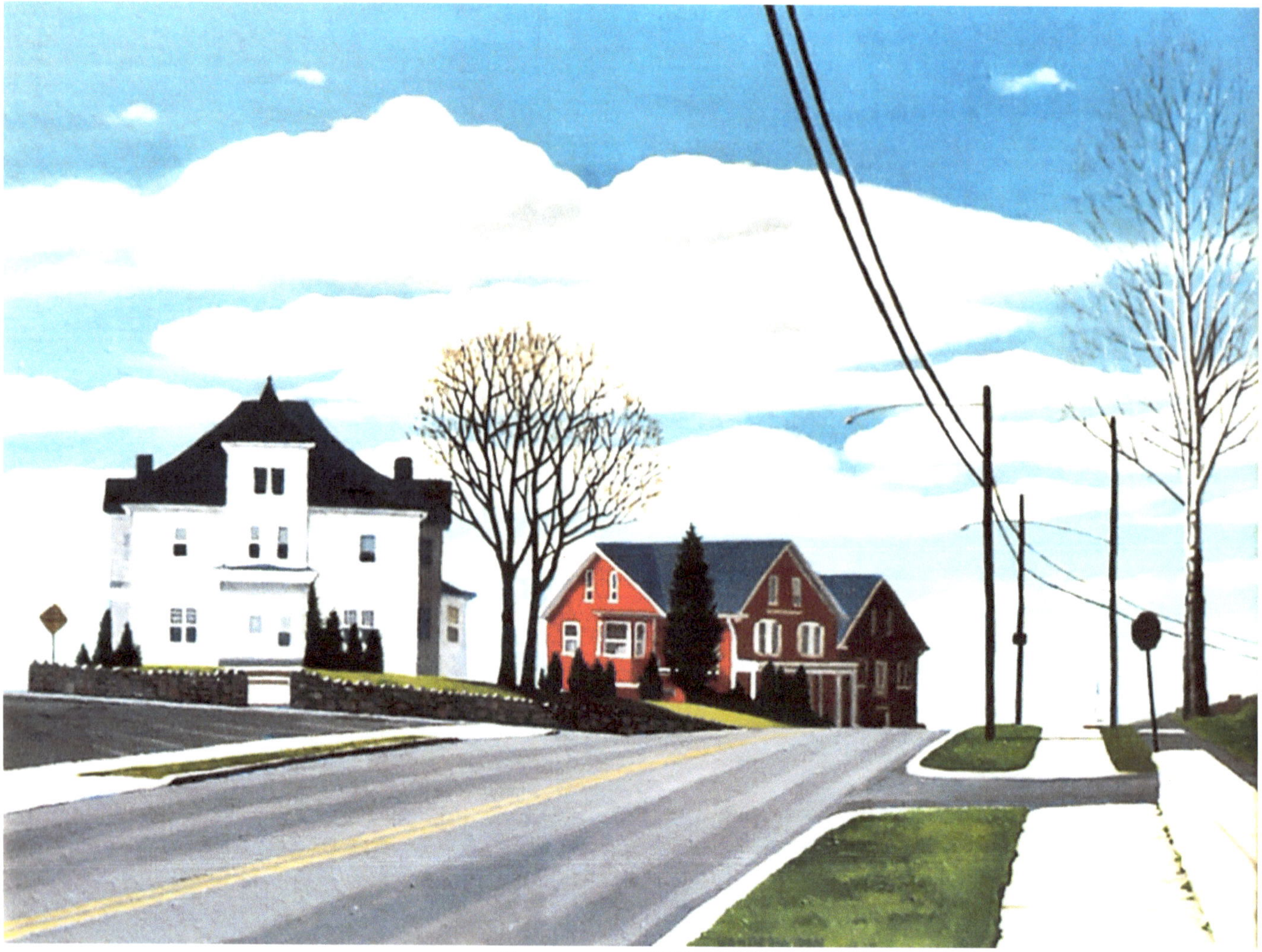

Houses on a Hill, 1988

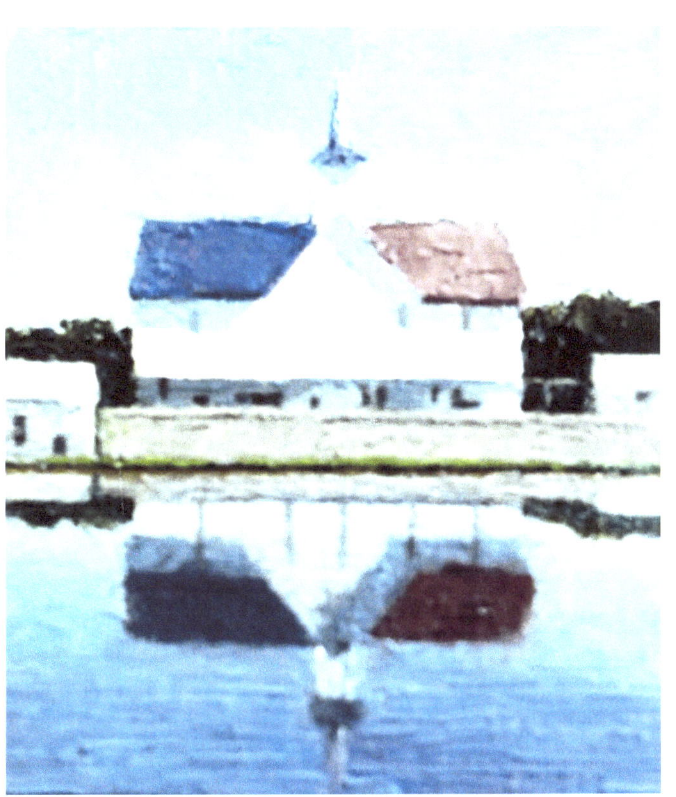
A View of the Star Barn, 2000

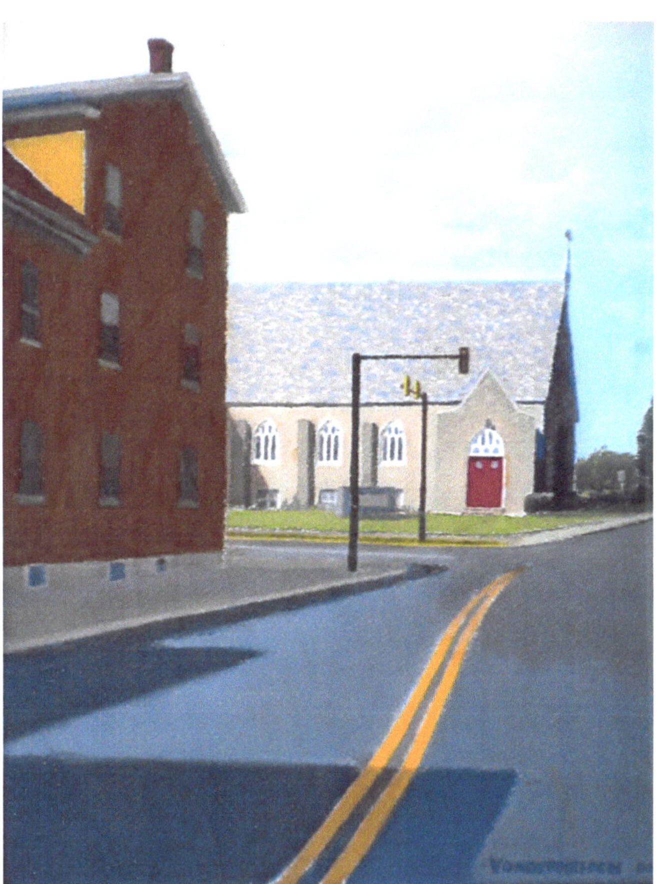
The Church Around the Corner, 2014

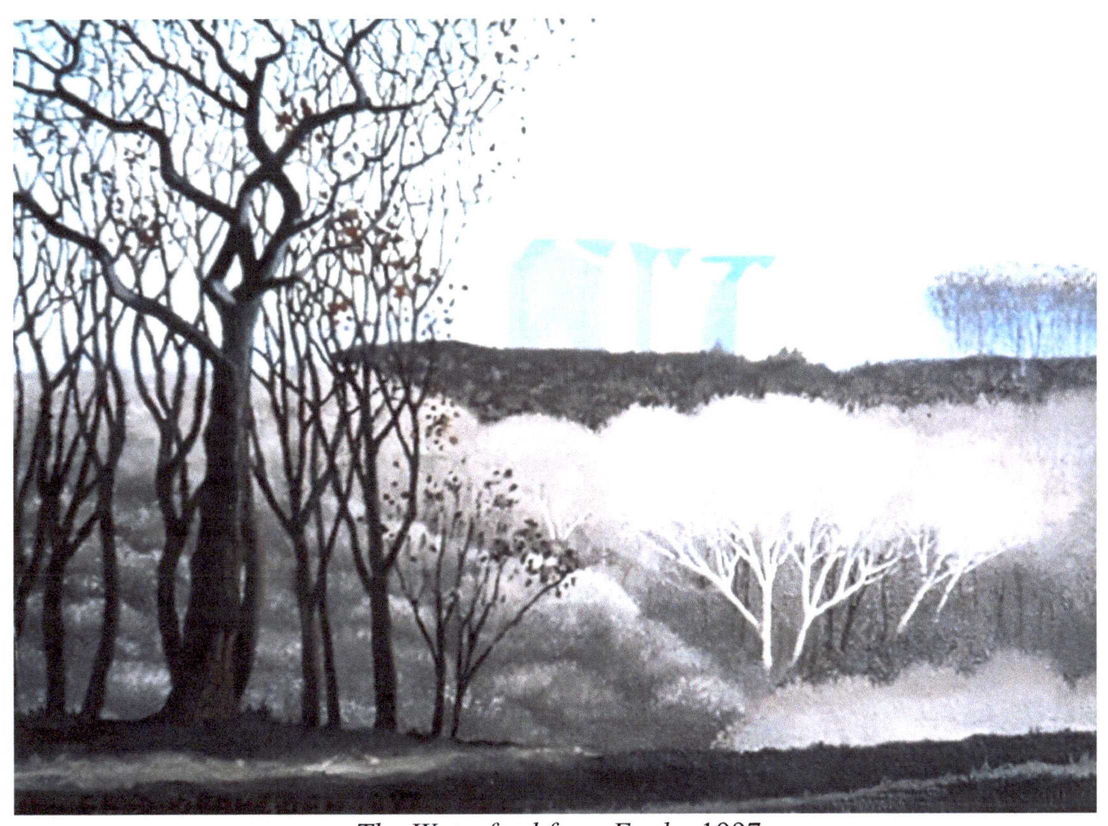
The Waterford from Enola, 1997

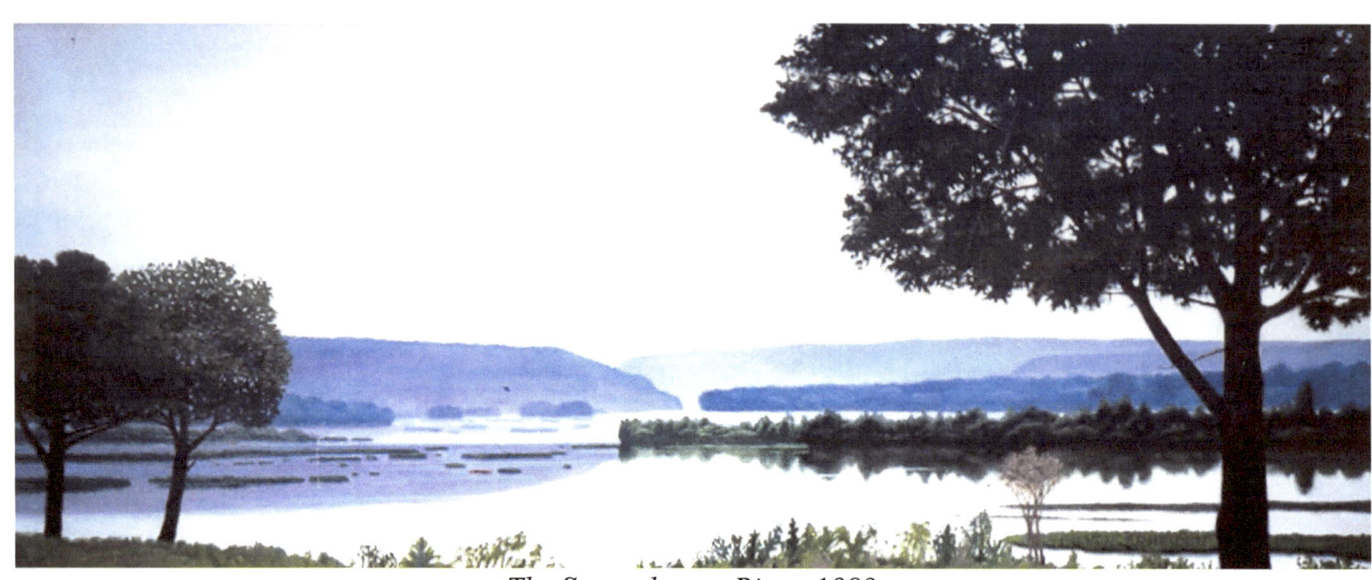

The Susquehanna River, 1989

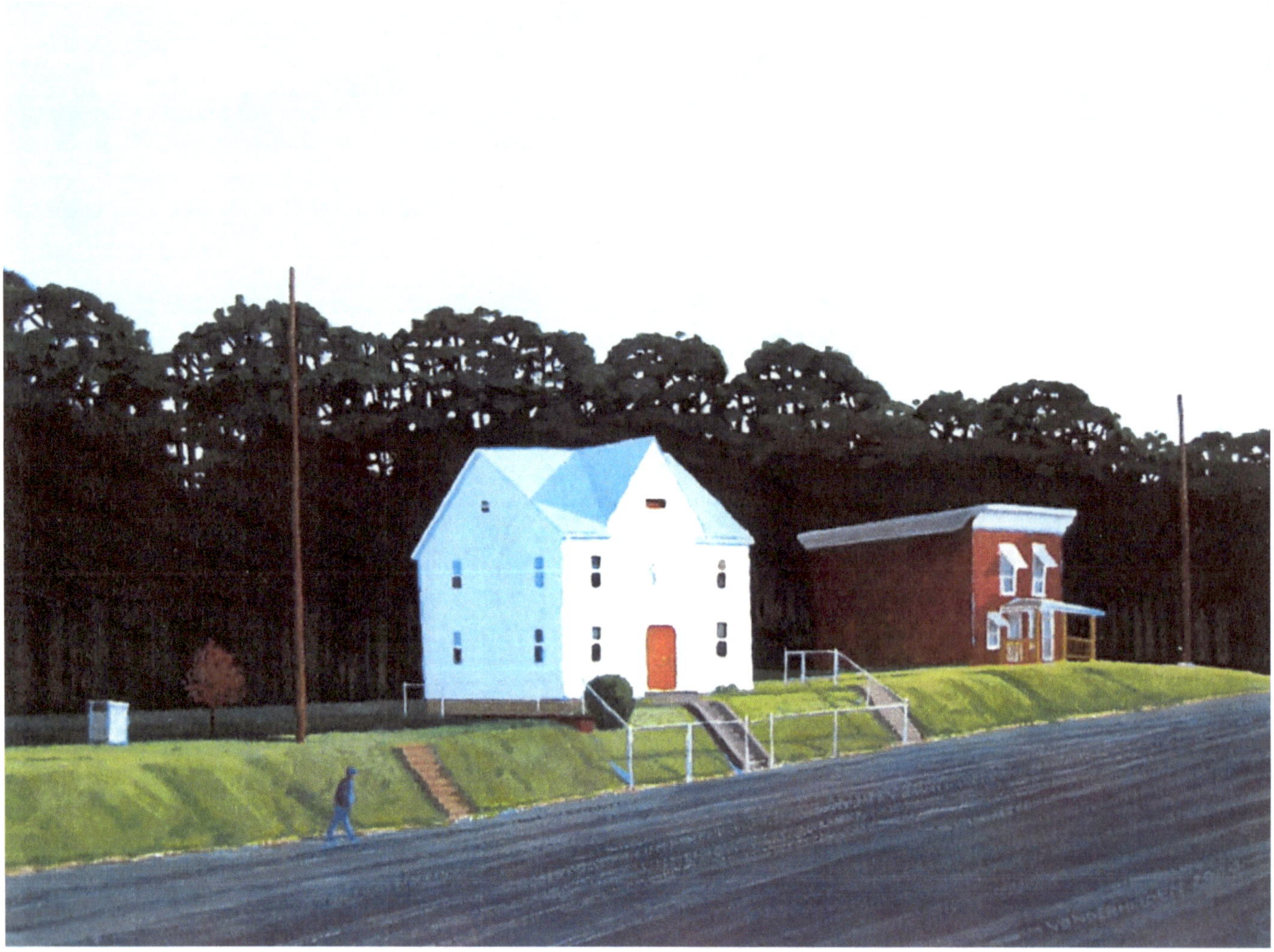

The Church with a Red Door, 2004

Portraits, Groups, and Figures

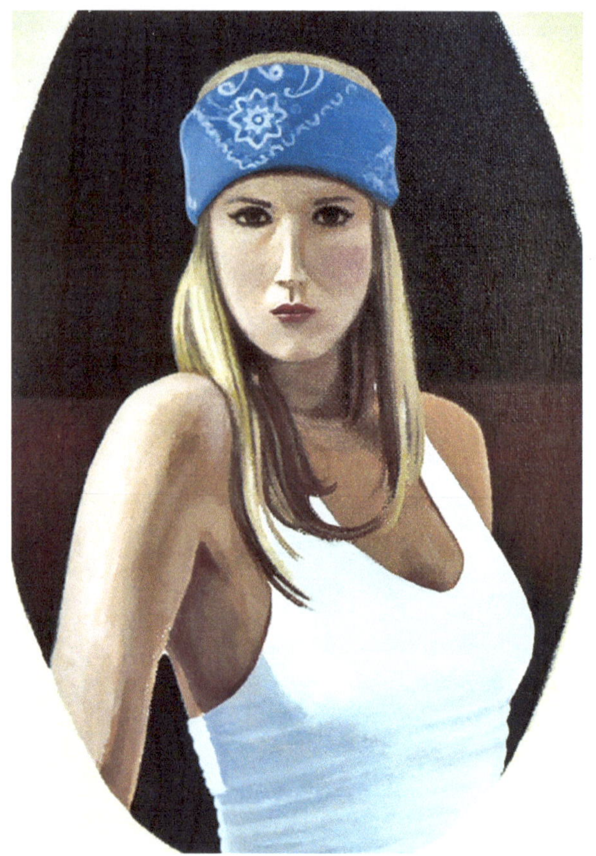

Girl with a Blue Bandana, 1998

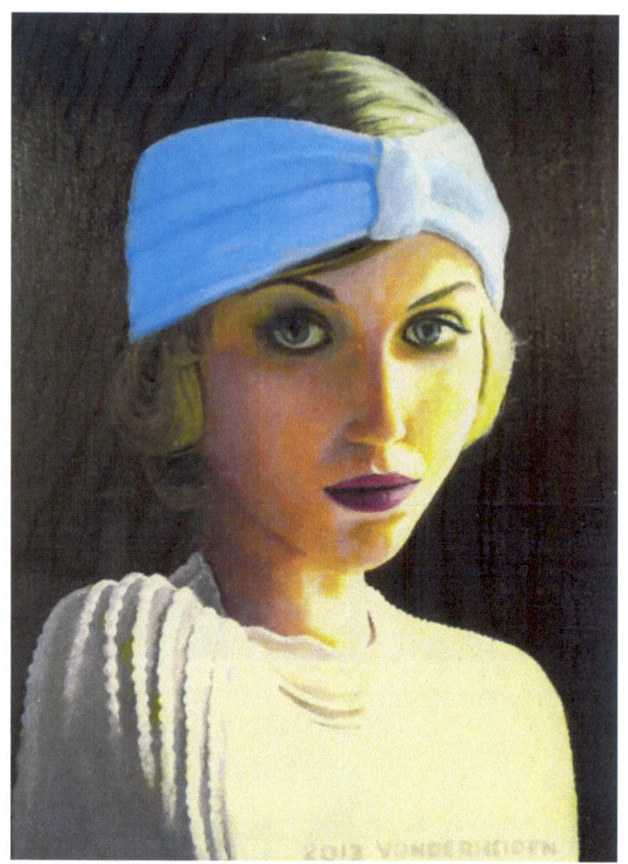

Daisy Buchanan, 2012

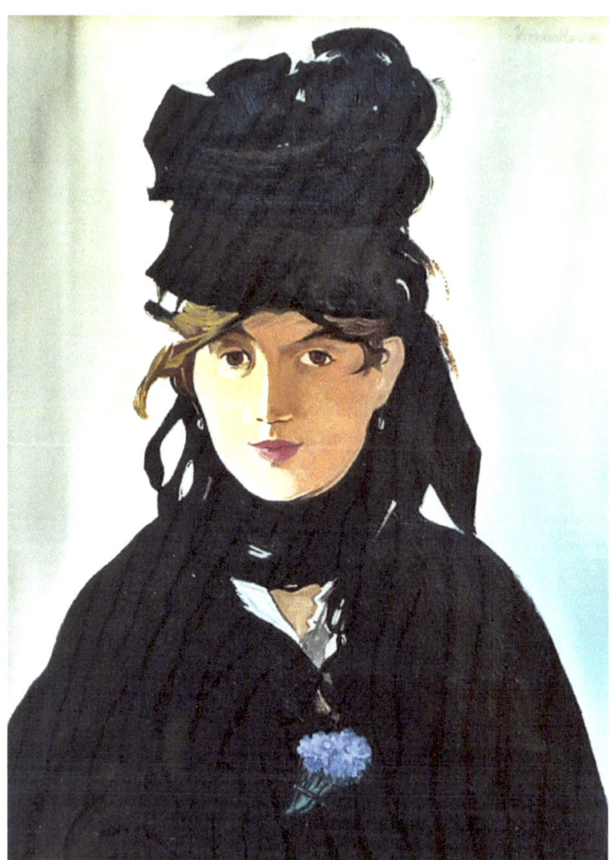

Berthe Morisot (after Manet), 2008

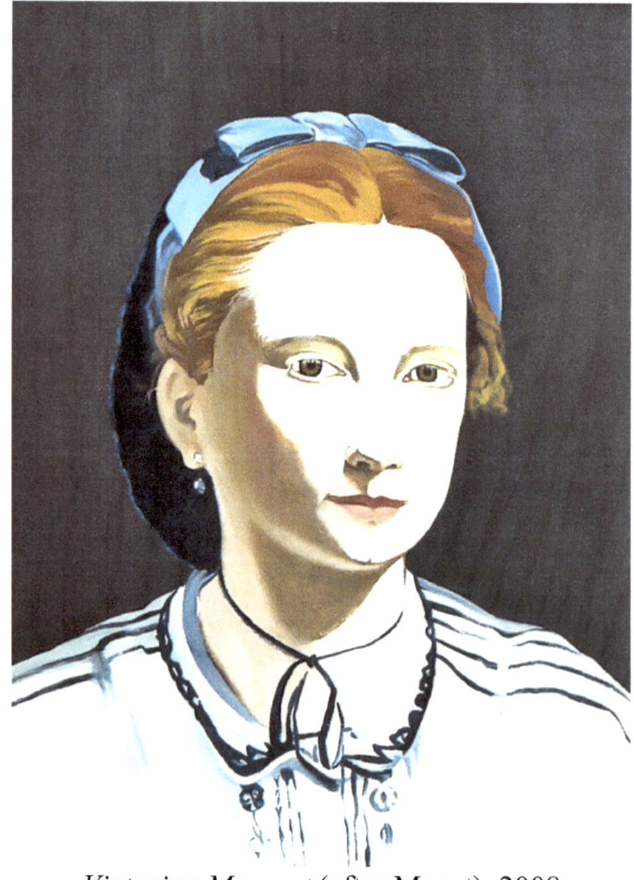

Victorine Meurent (after Manet), 2008

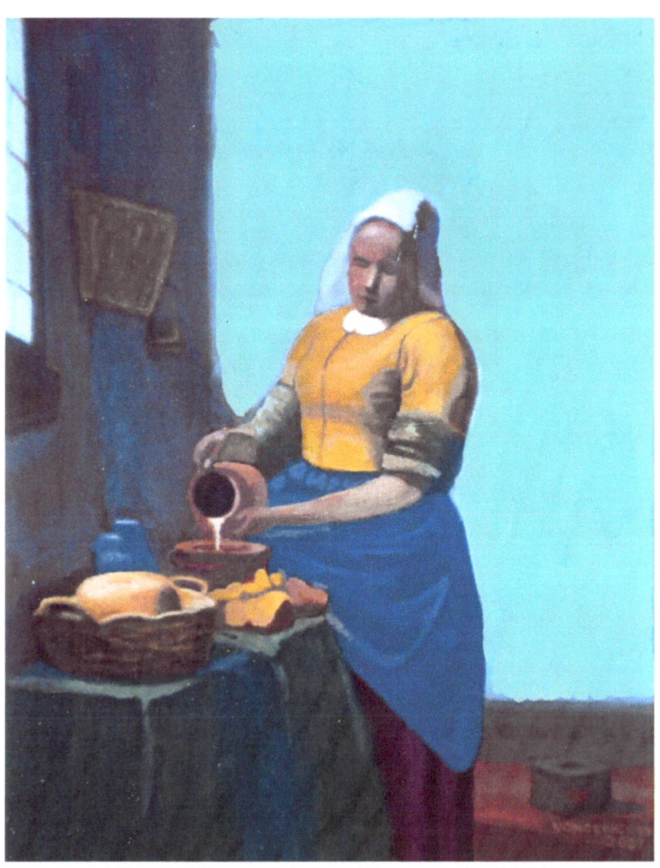

The Milkmaid (after Vermeer), 2007

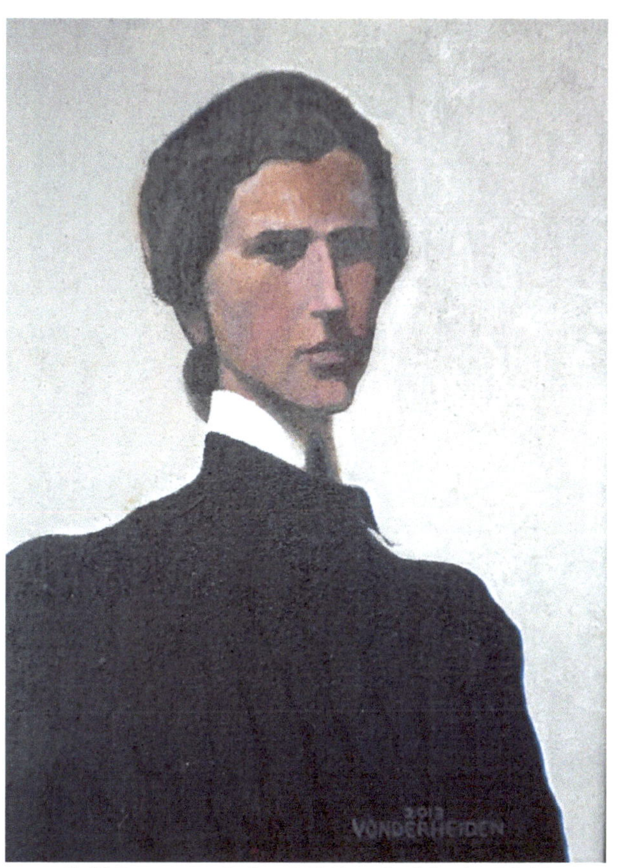

Self Portrait (after Violet Oakley), 2013

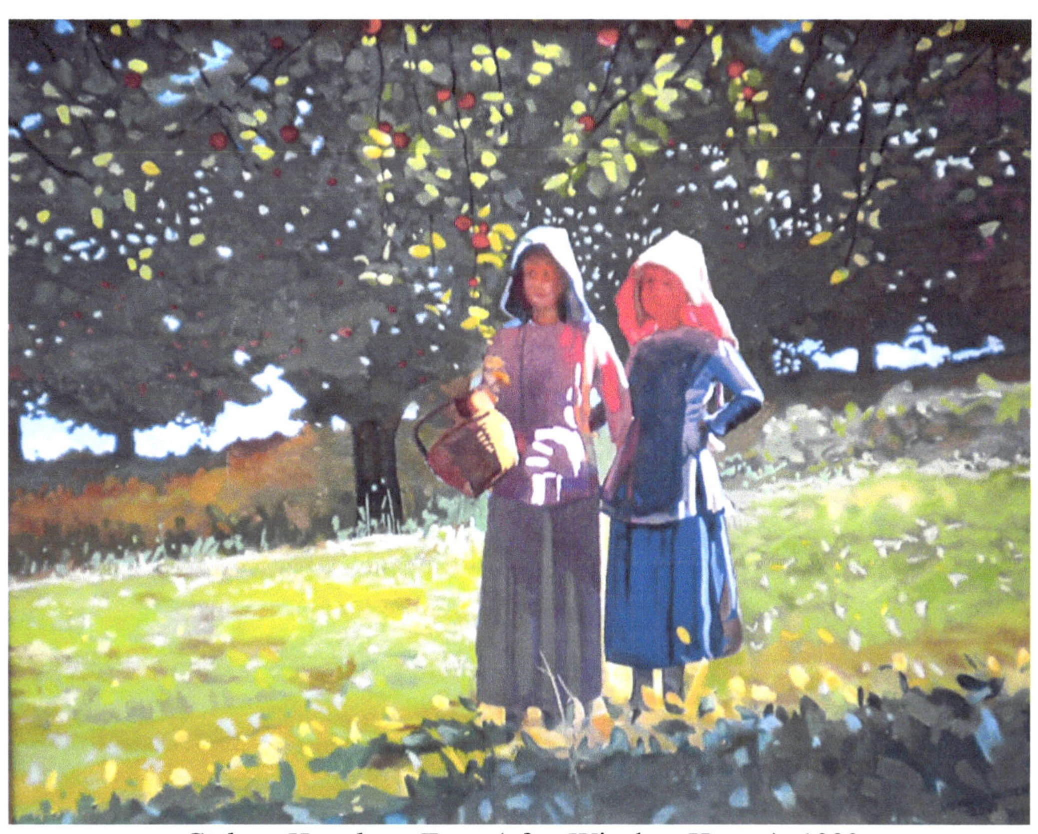

Girls at Houghton Farm (after Winslow Homer), 1999

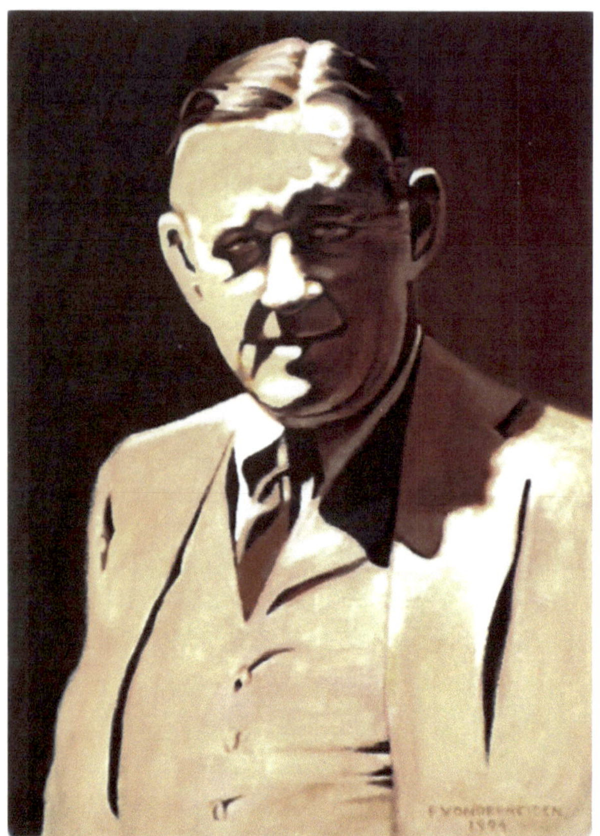

John O'Hara, 1994

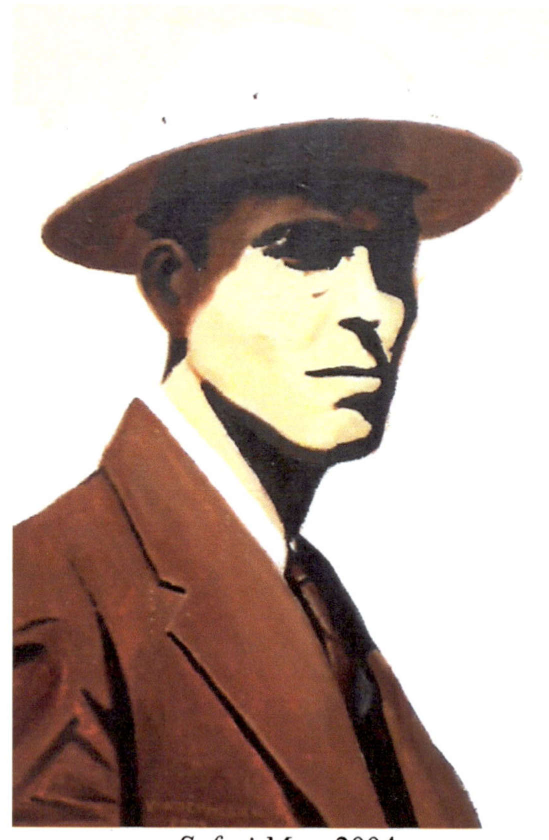

Safari Man, 2004

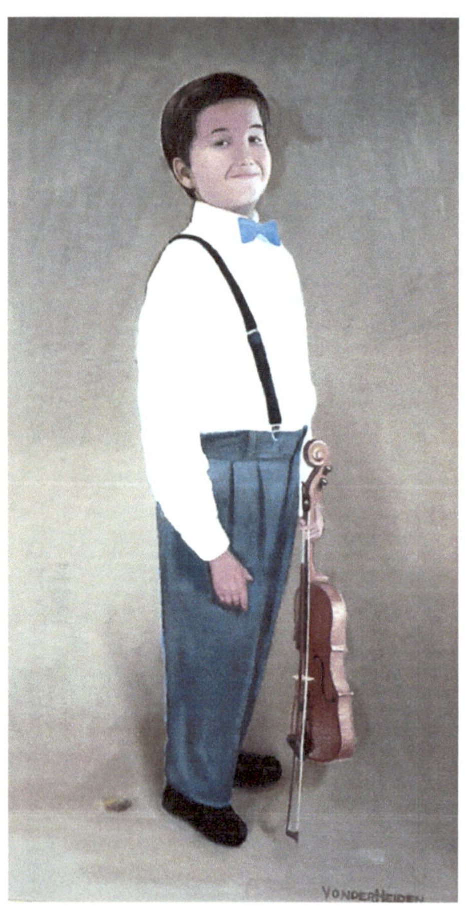

The Prodigy, 2007

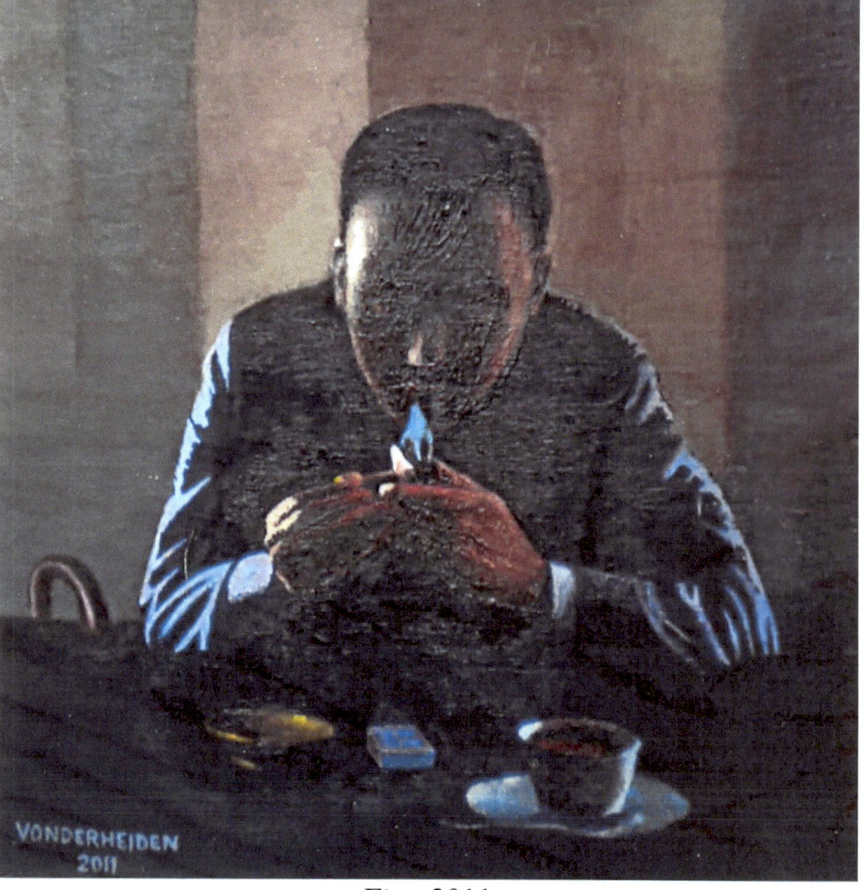

Fire, 2011

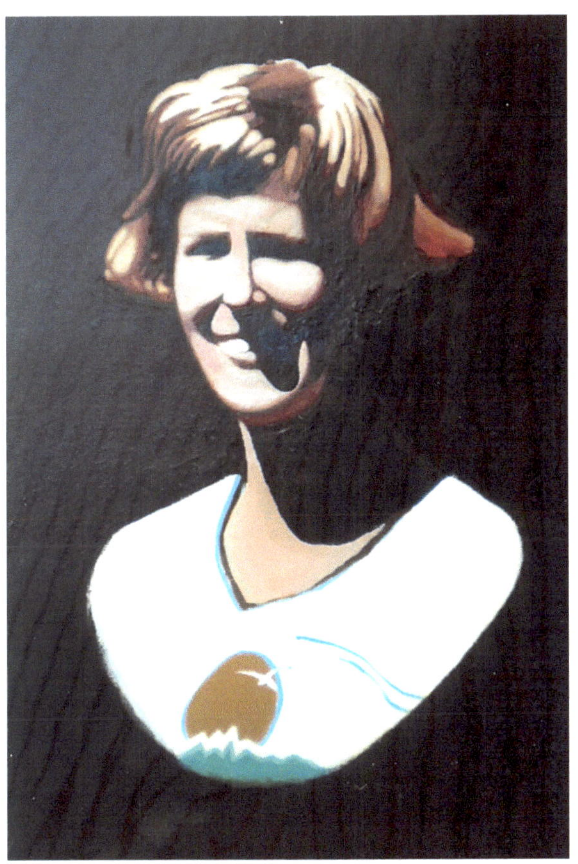
(Young) Marilyn in Aruba, 1996

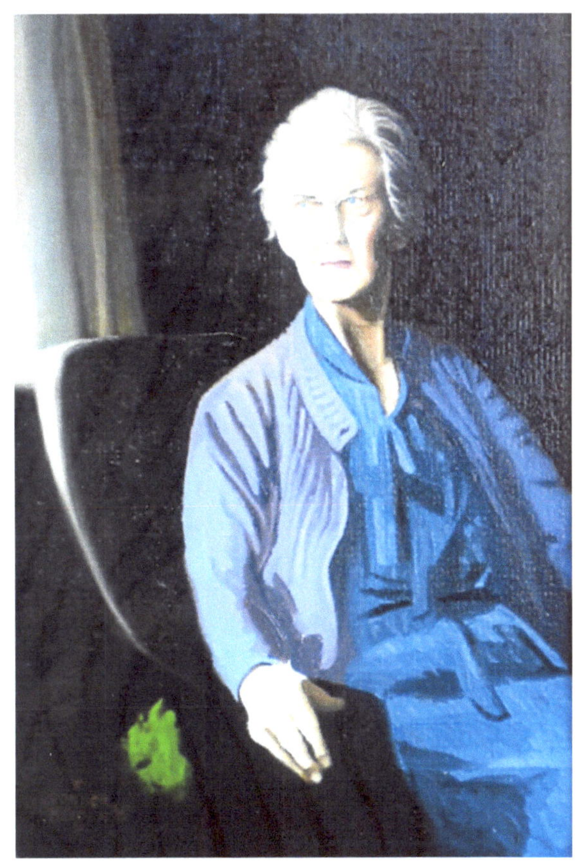
(Mom) Mary Kraus, 1998

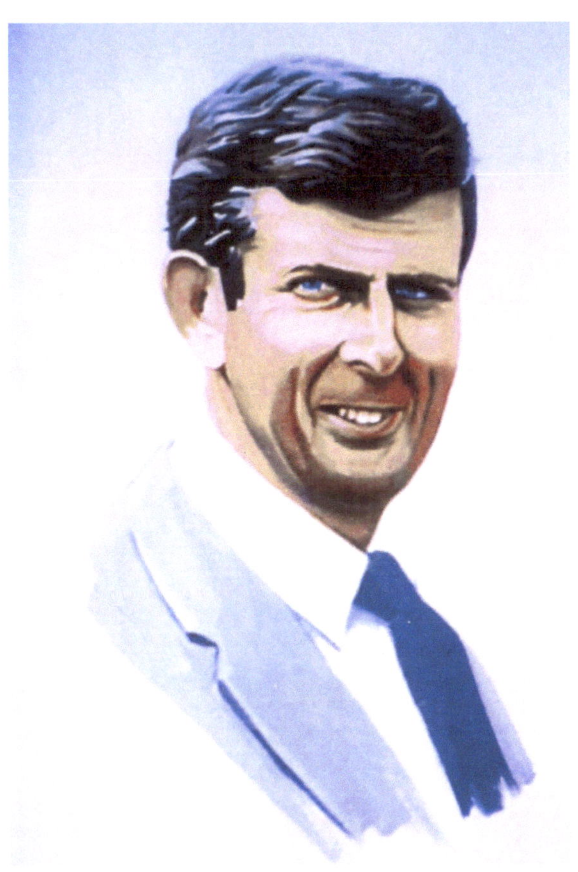
Bill Kraus, 1990

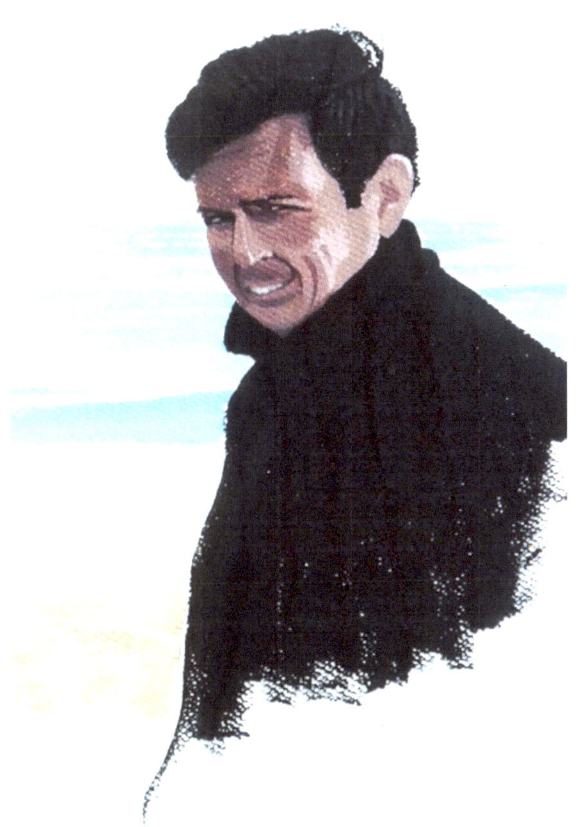
Bill at the Beach, 1999

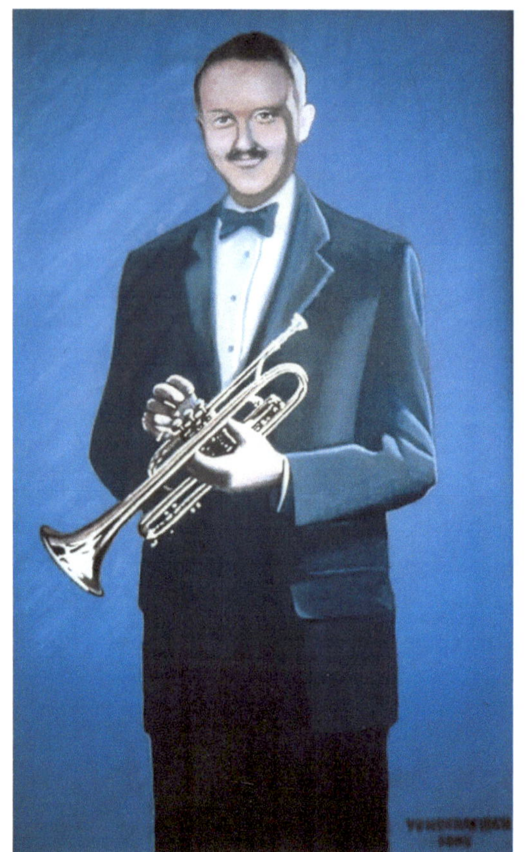
Bix Beiderbecke, 1997

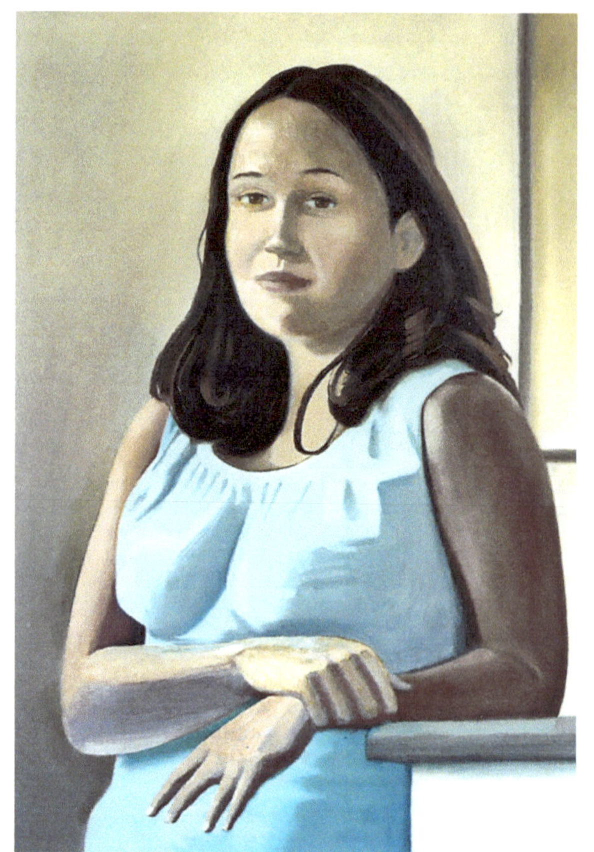
Elena, 1998

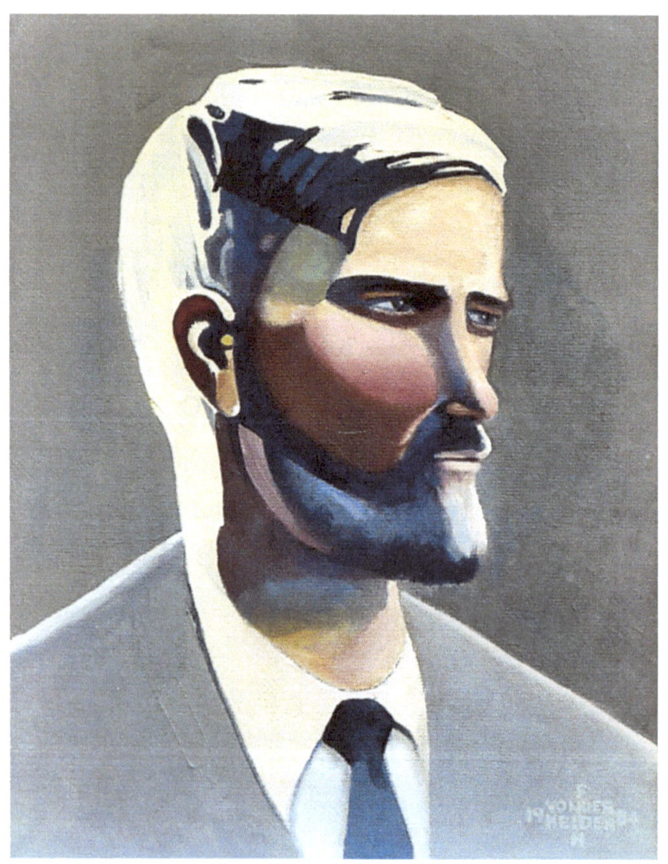
Rainbow Man, 1984

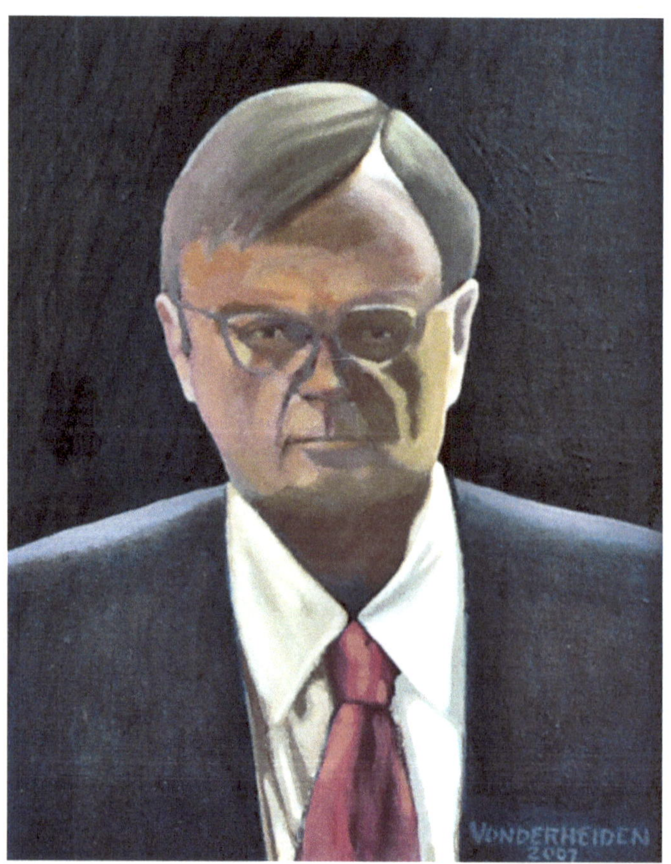

Radio Man, 2007

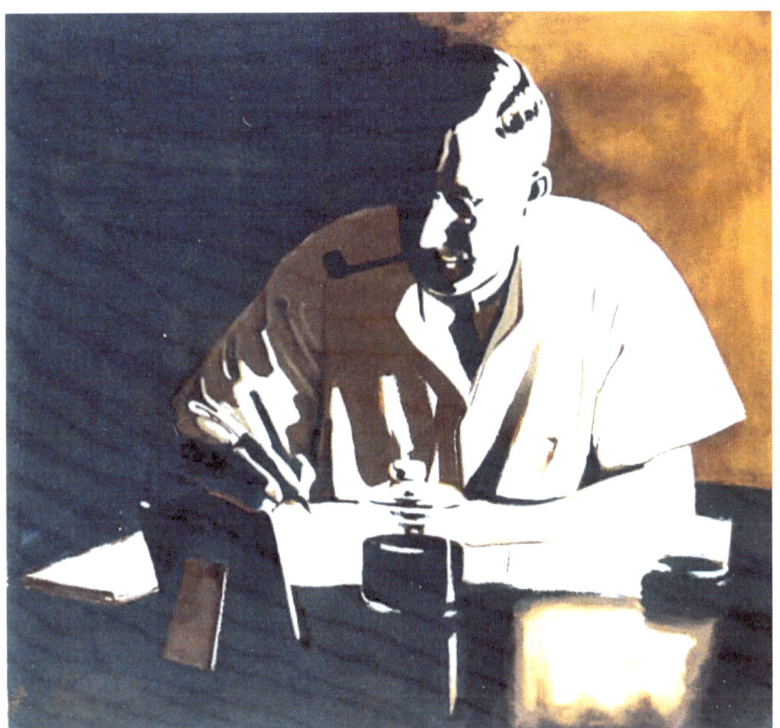

The Researcher, 2009

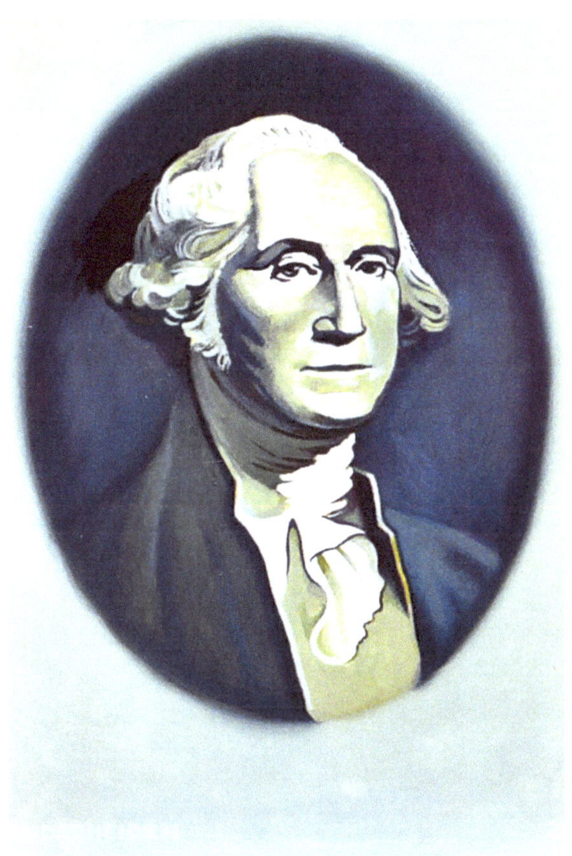

The Father of His Country, 1995

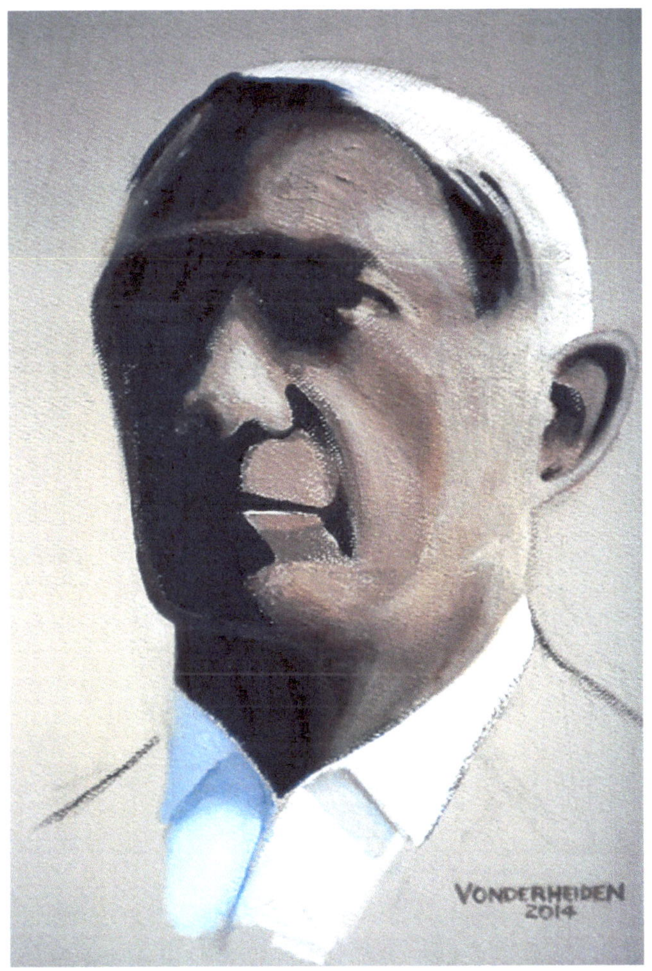

Homo Pictor Neanderthalensis Hispanicus, 2014

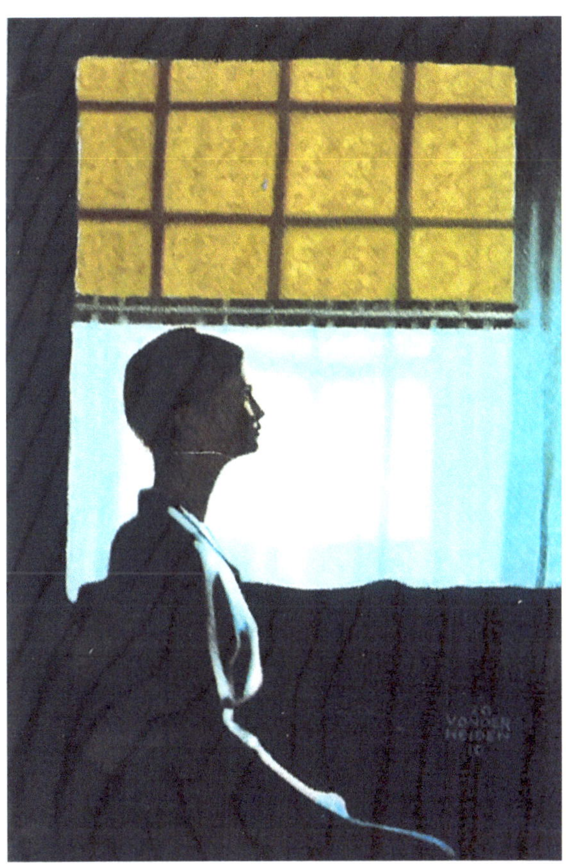

Arrangement in Blue & Gold, 2010

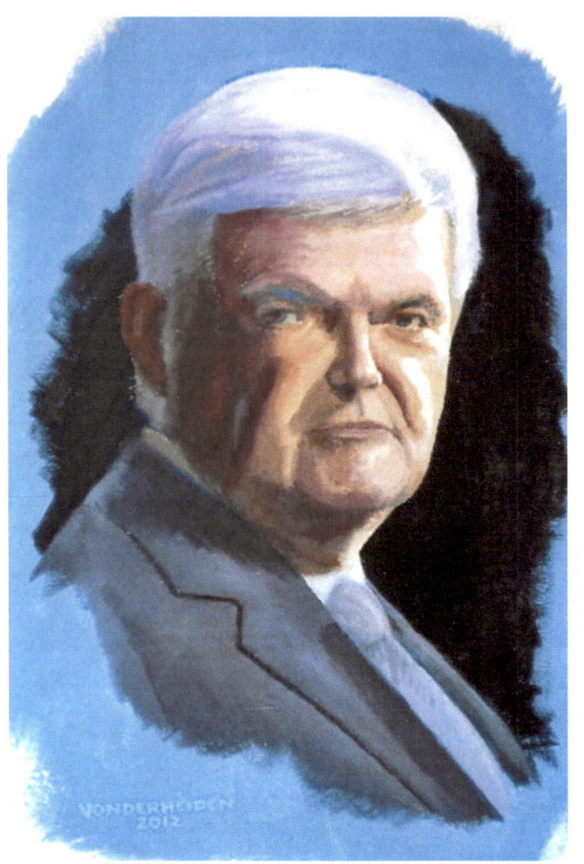

The Elderly Candidate, 2012

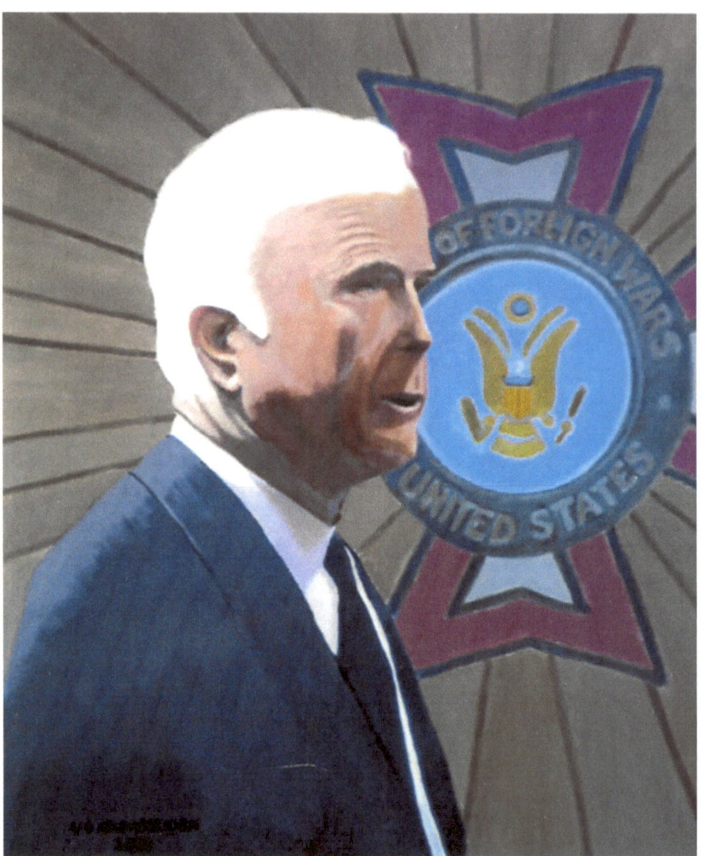

The Veteran Candidate, 2009

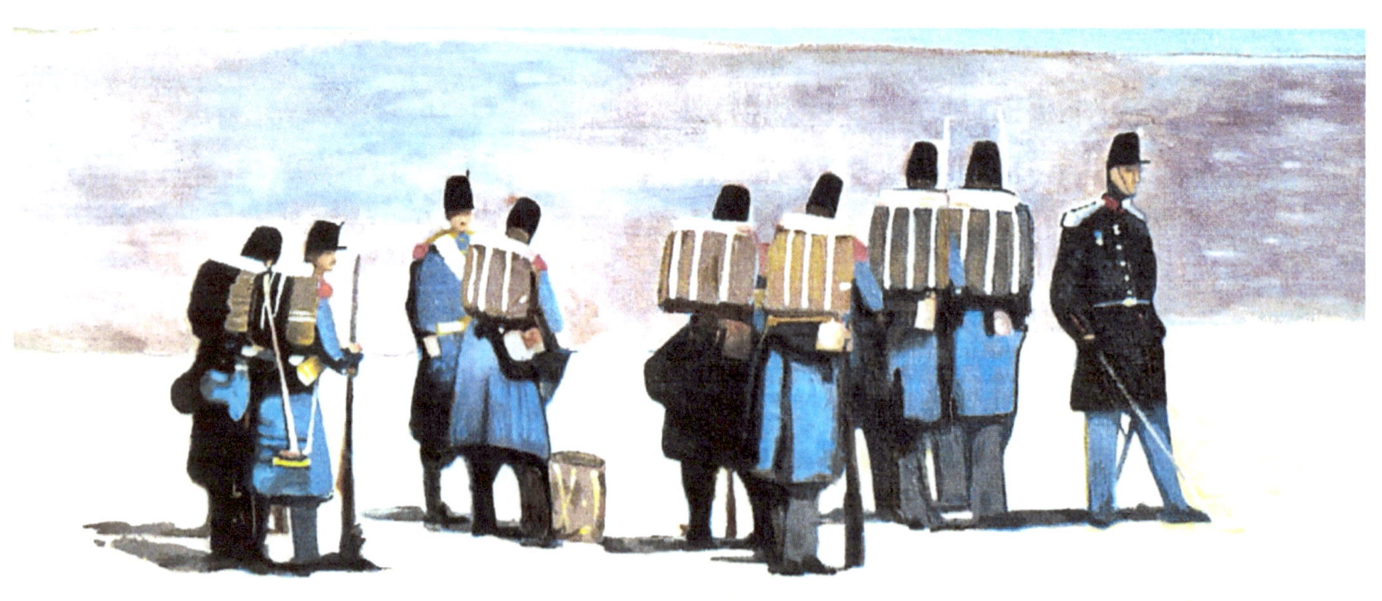

VONDERHEIDEN
2006

French Soldiers (after Fattori), 2006

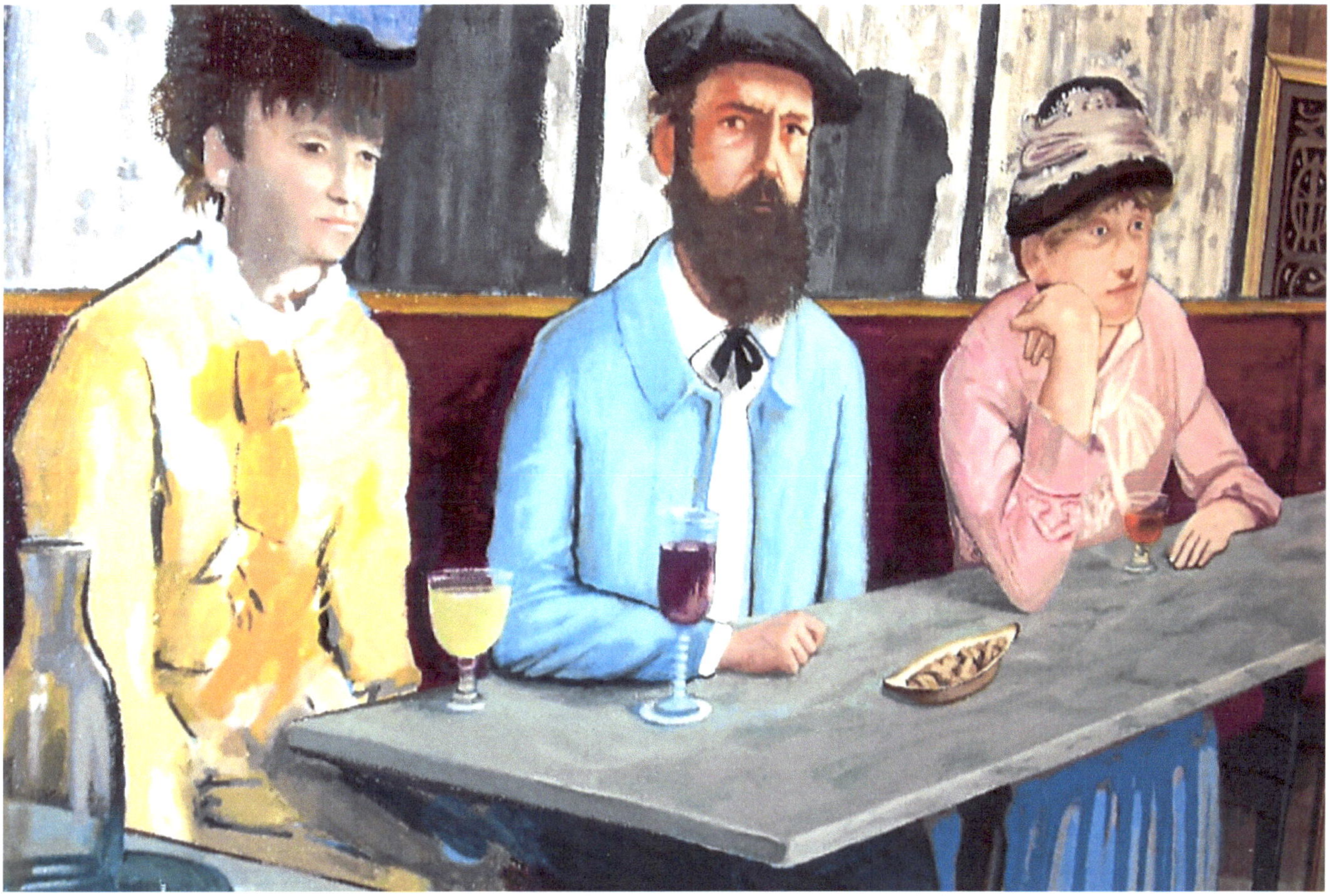

The Happy Hour (after Degas, Monet & Manet), 2010

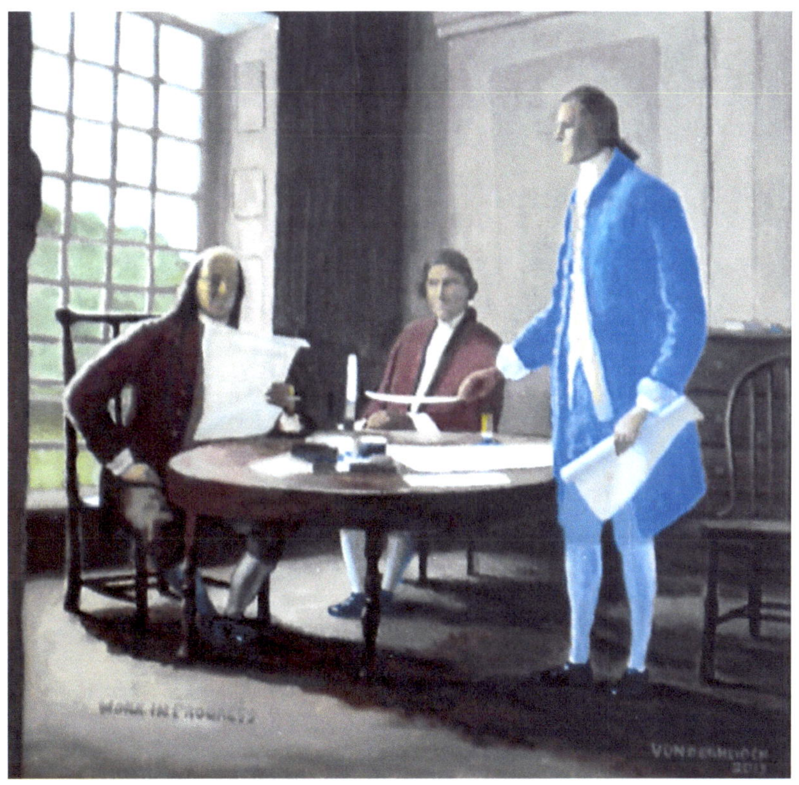

Work in Progress (after Ferris), 2013

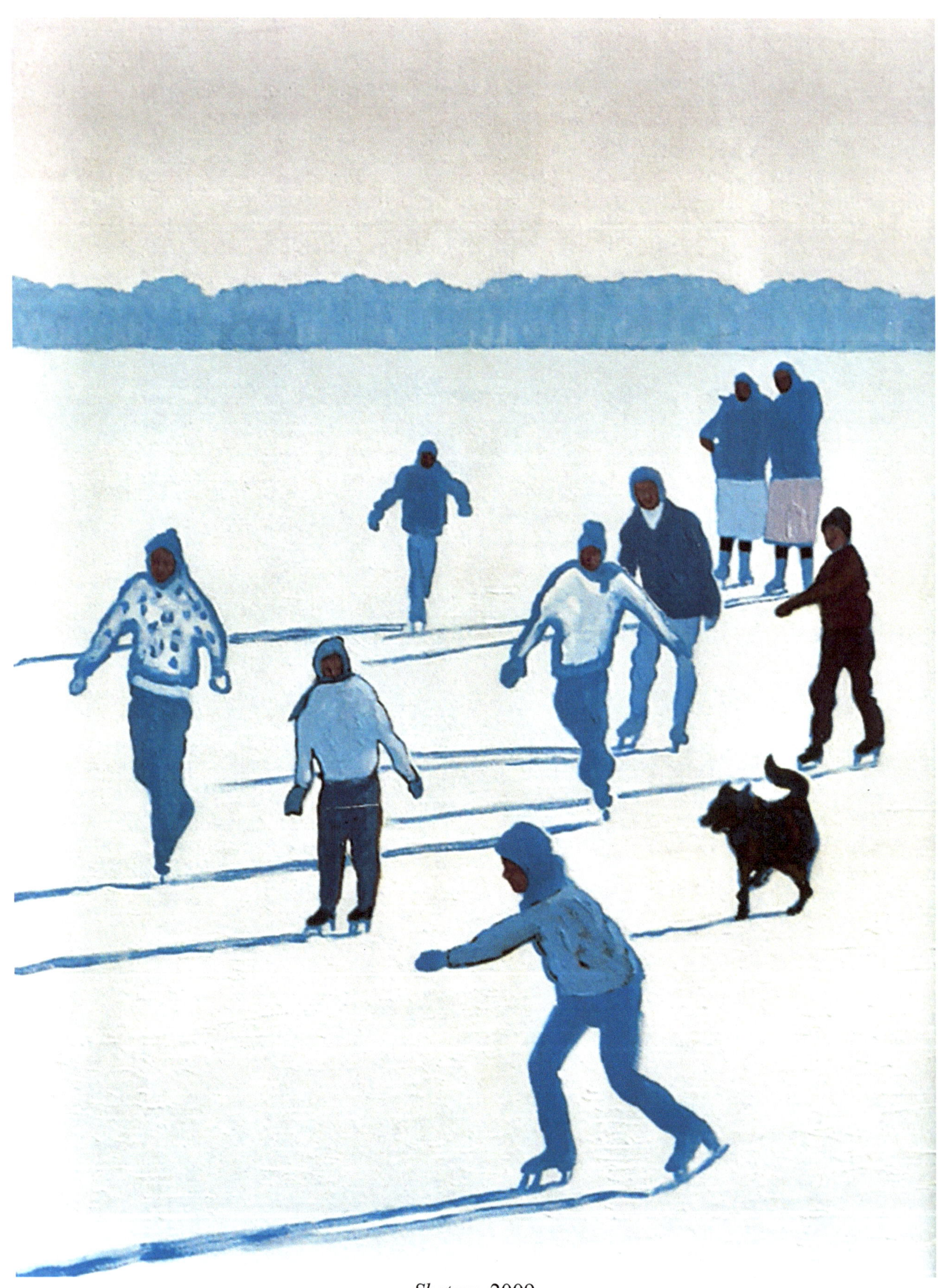

Skaters, 2009

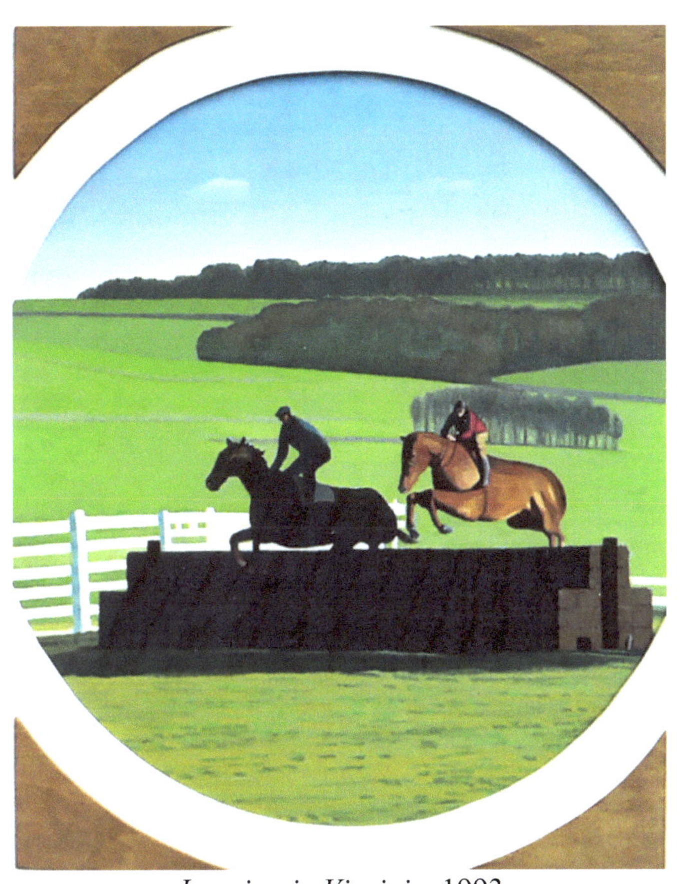

Jumping in Virginia, 1993

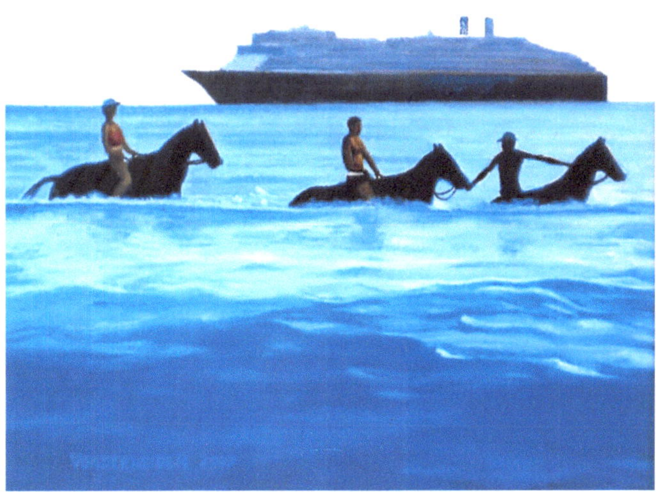

Riding at Aruba, 2009

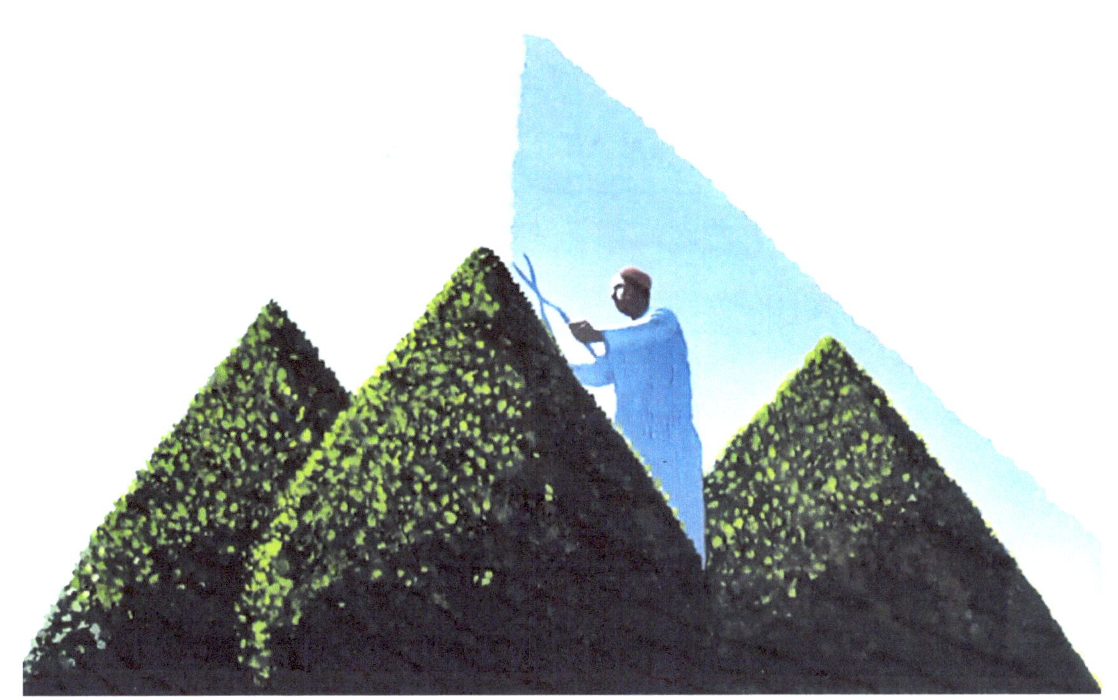

In the Gardens of Giza, 1998

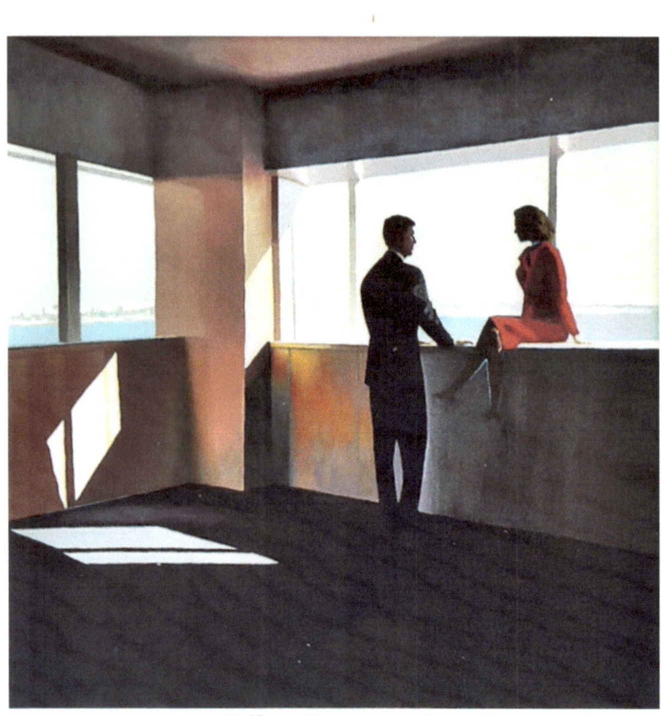

Office Space, 1996

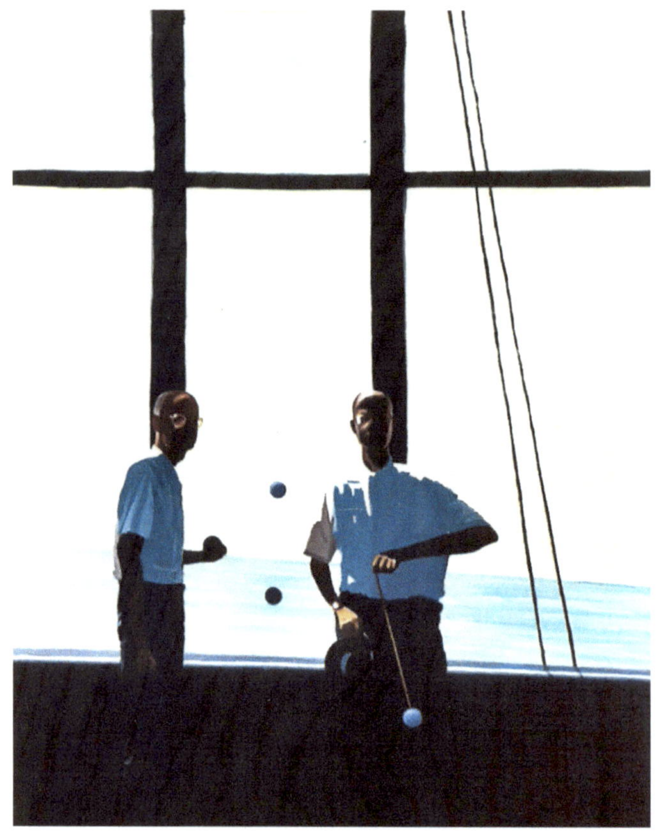

Verifying Gravity, 2008

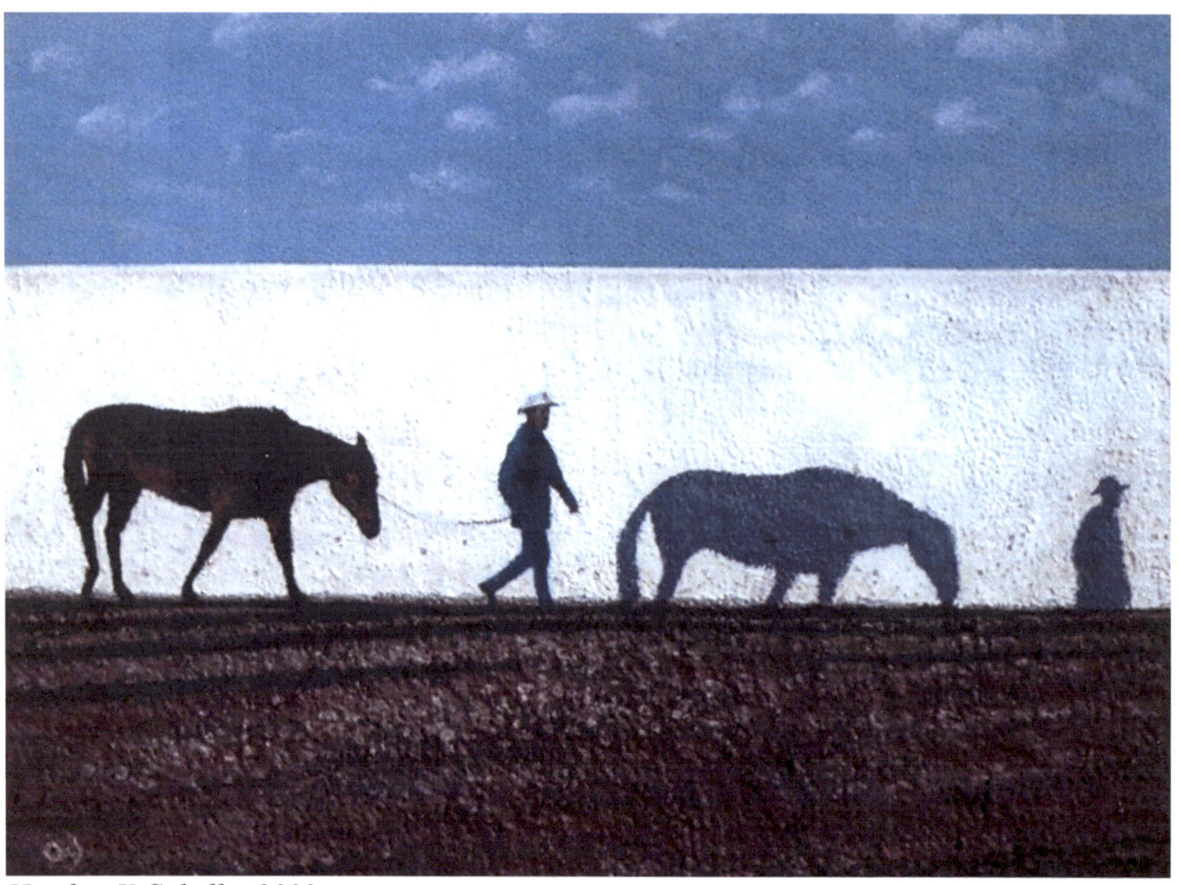

Hombre Y Cabello, 2002

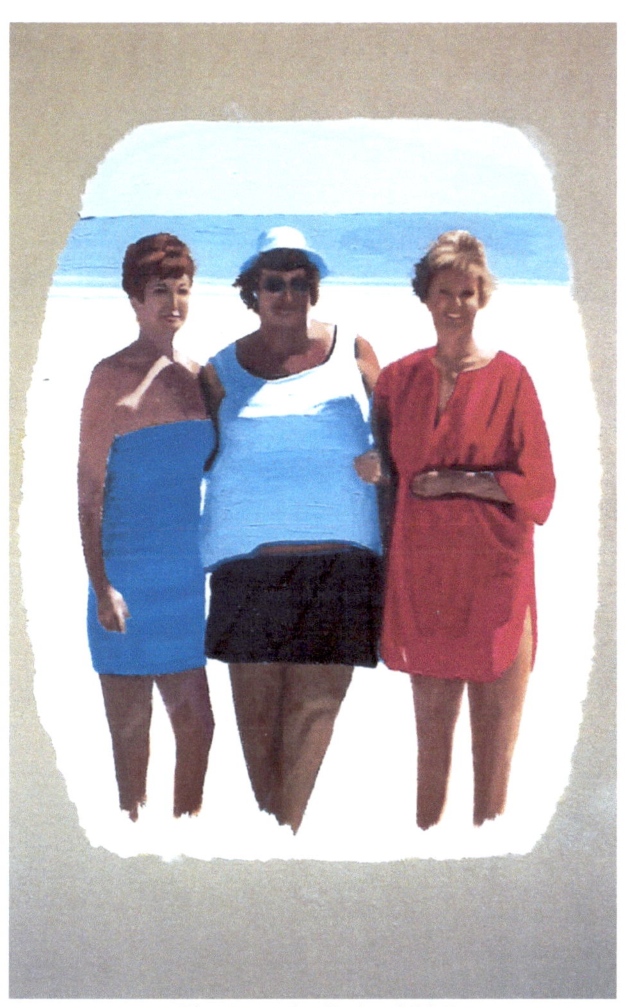

The Beach Girls, 2007

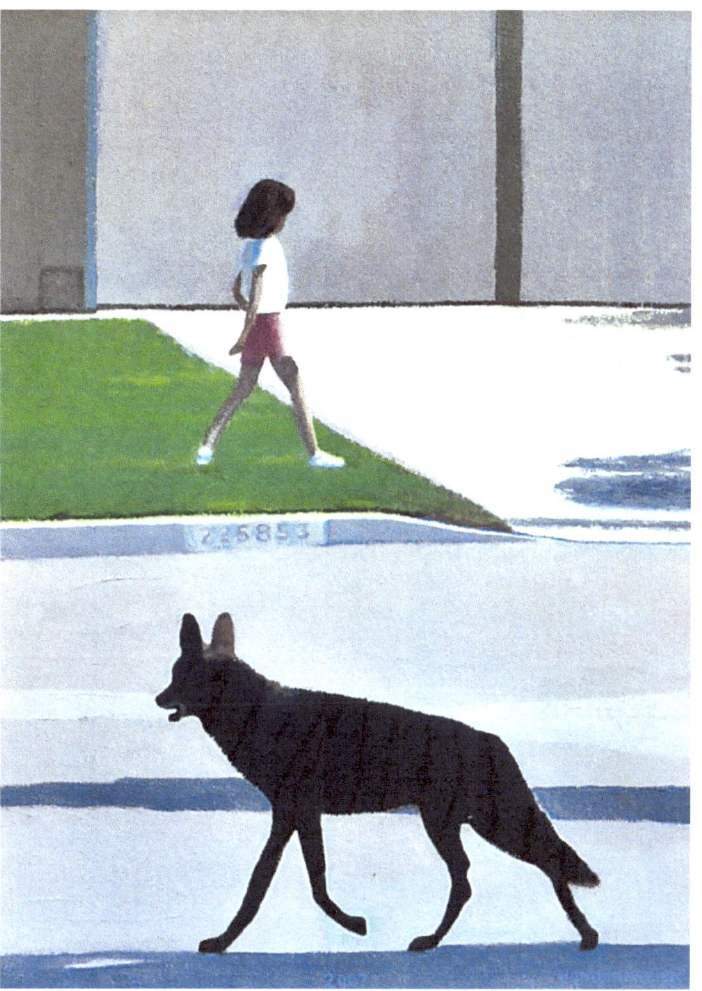

Urban Intruder, 2004

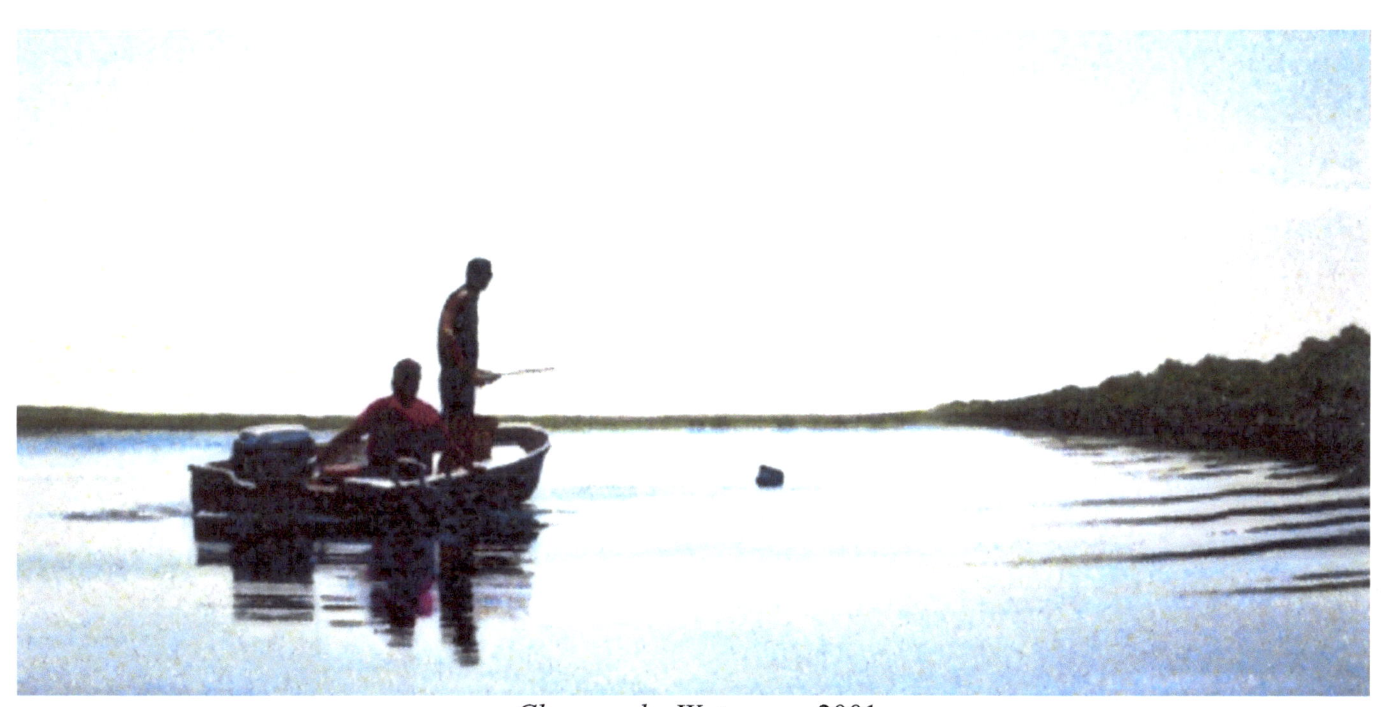

Chesapeake Watermen, 2001

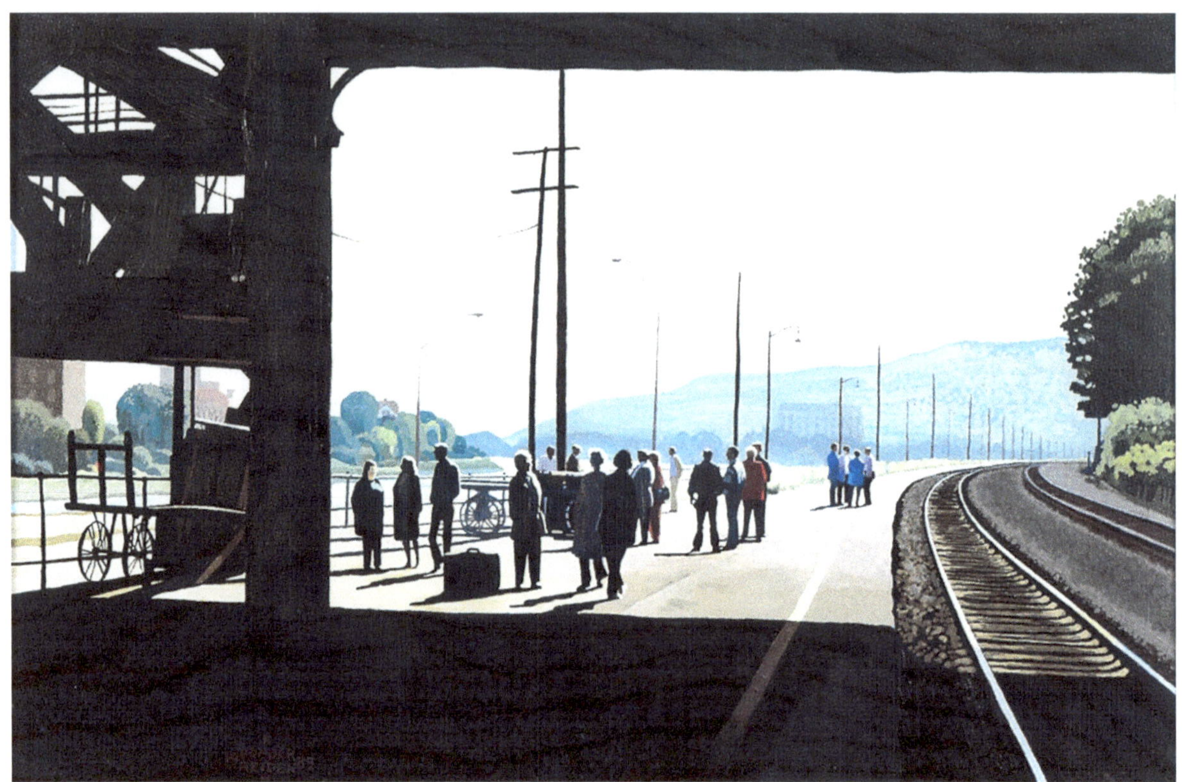

Station Break, 1989

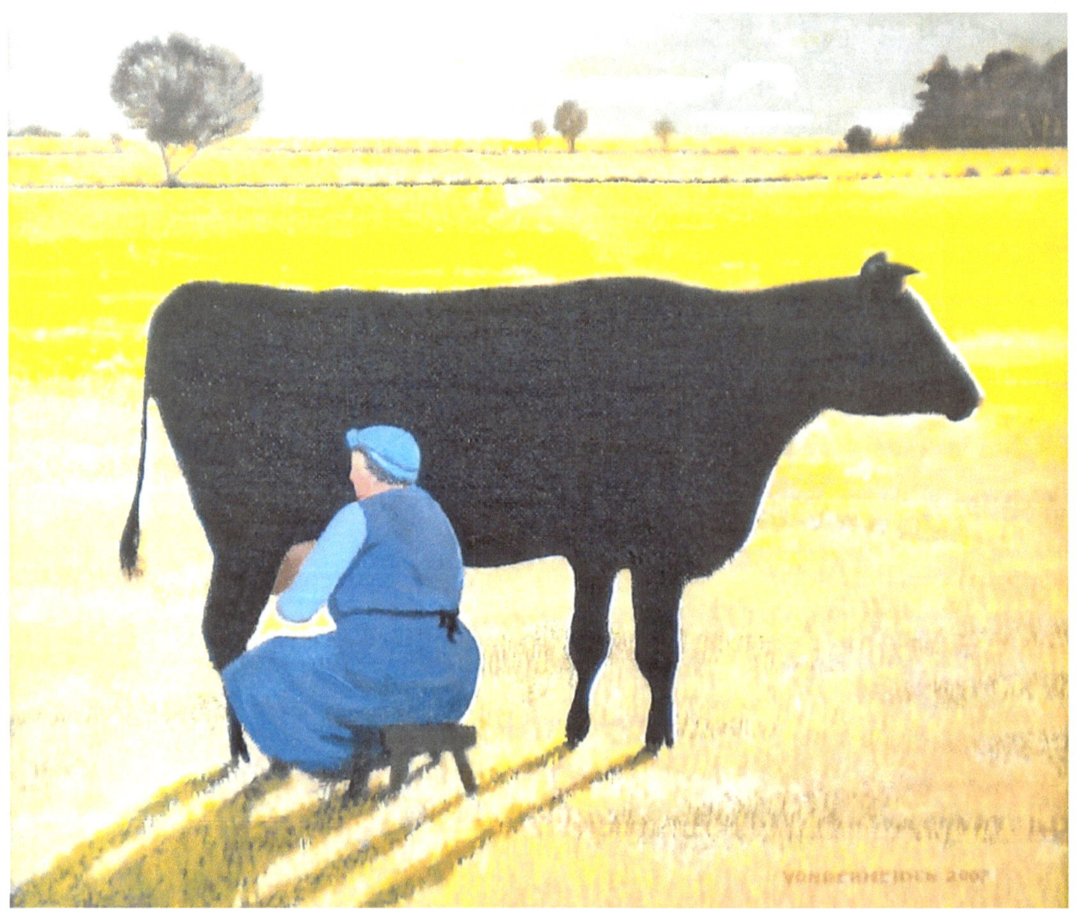

Milking in the Field, 2007

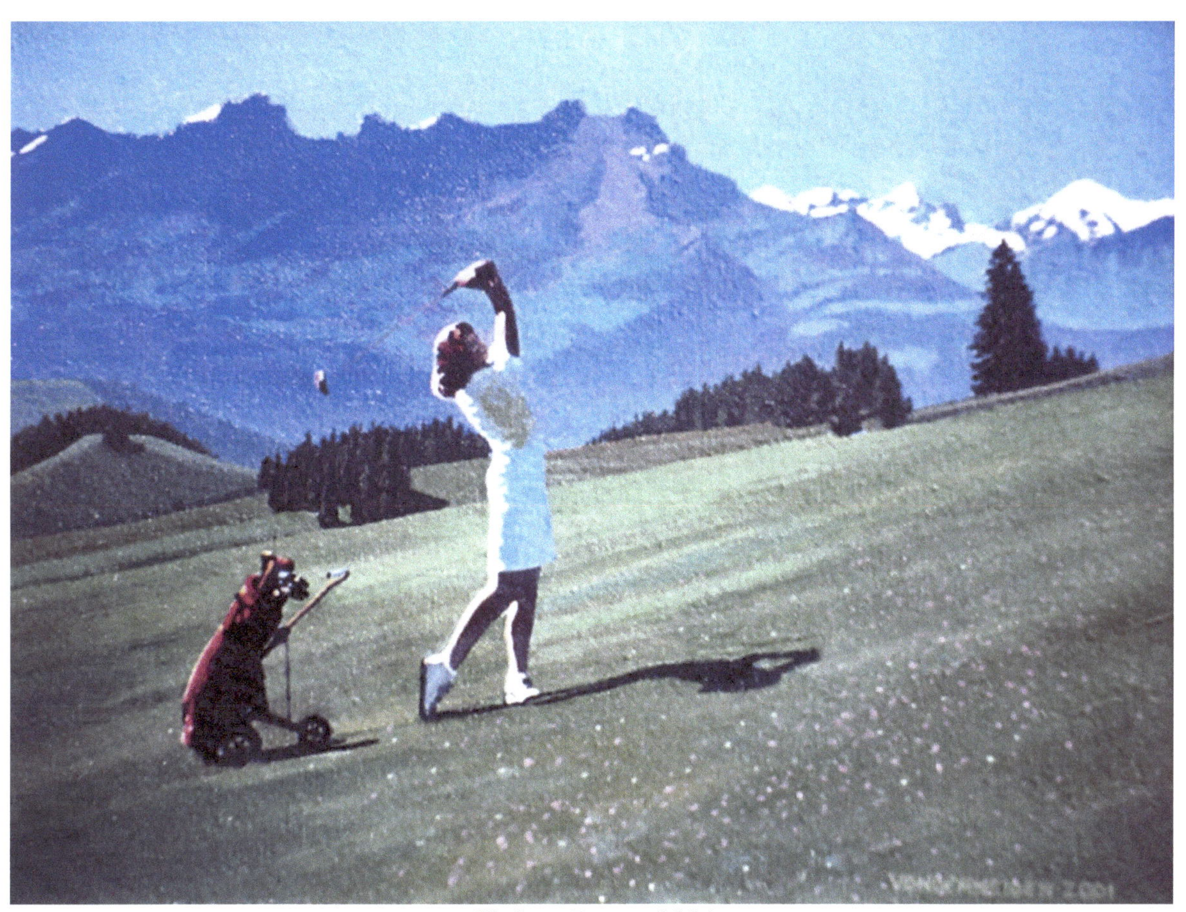

Skyline Drive, 2001

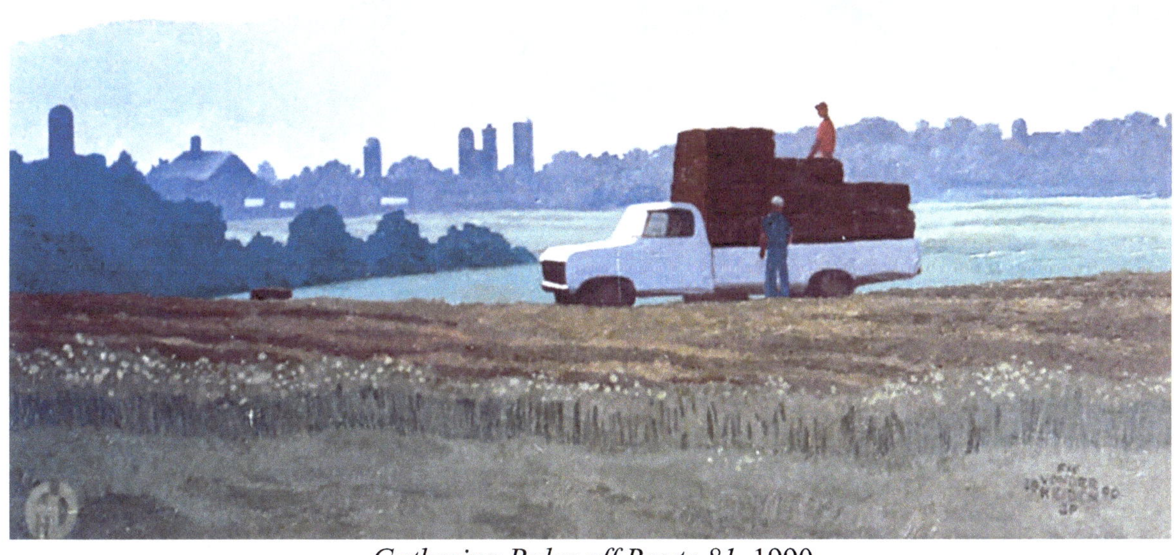

Gathering Bales off Route 81, 1990

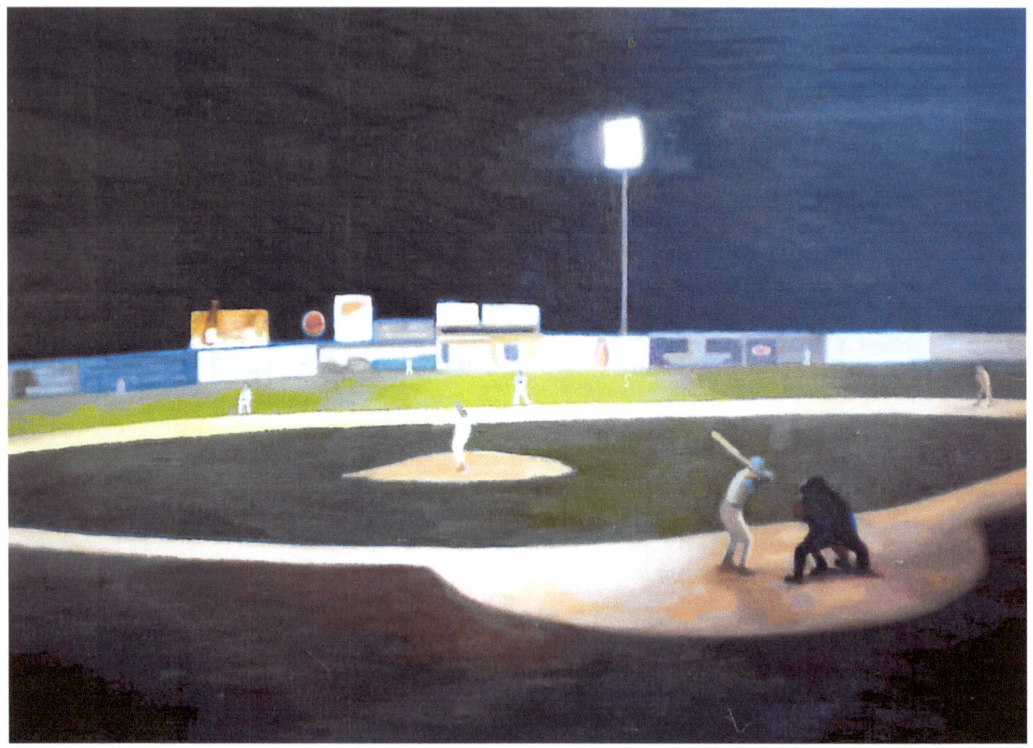

Night Game, 2009

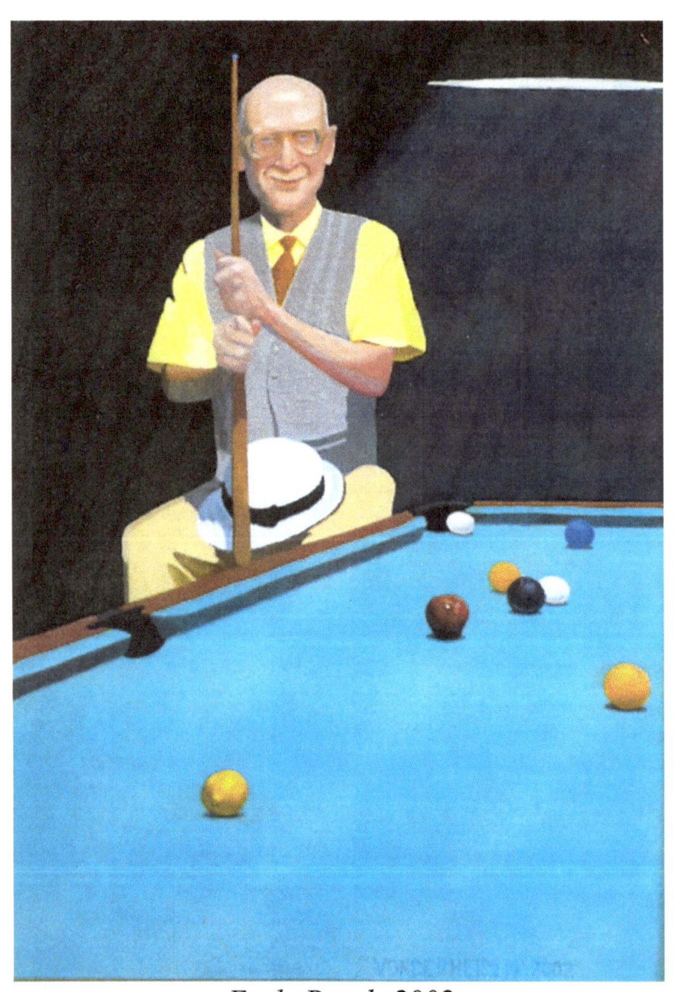

Early Break, 2002

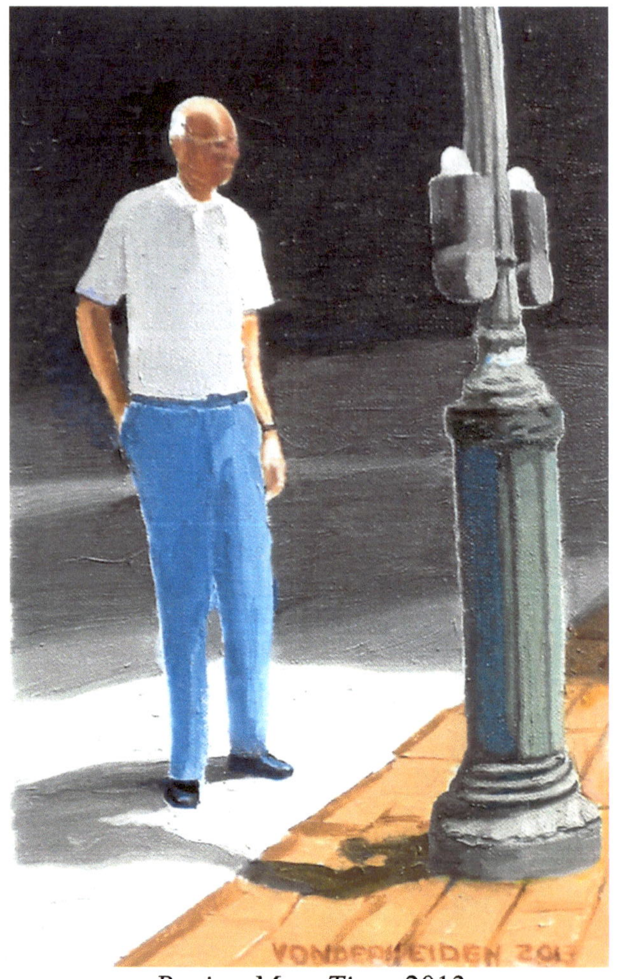

Buying More Time, 2013

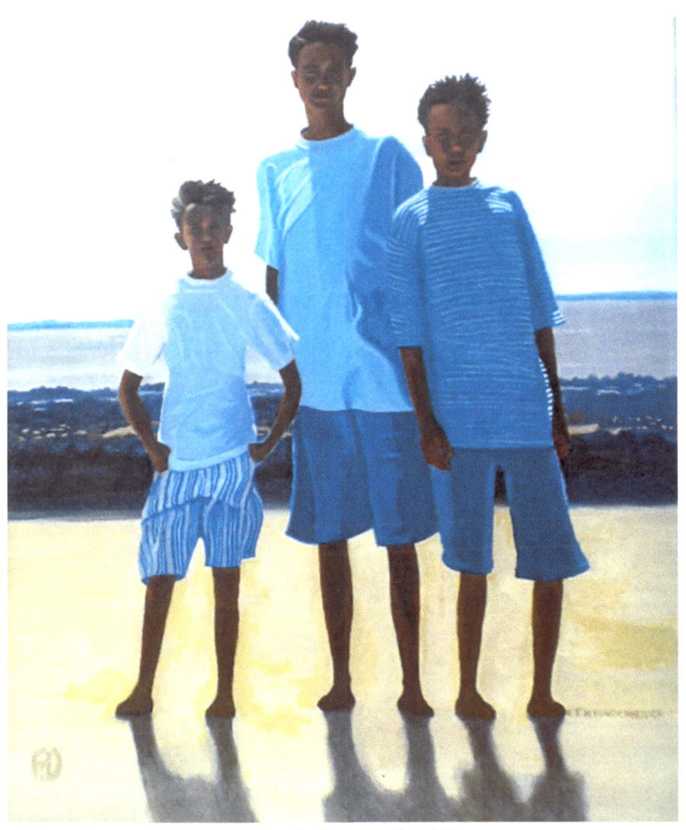

Beach Boys, 2010

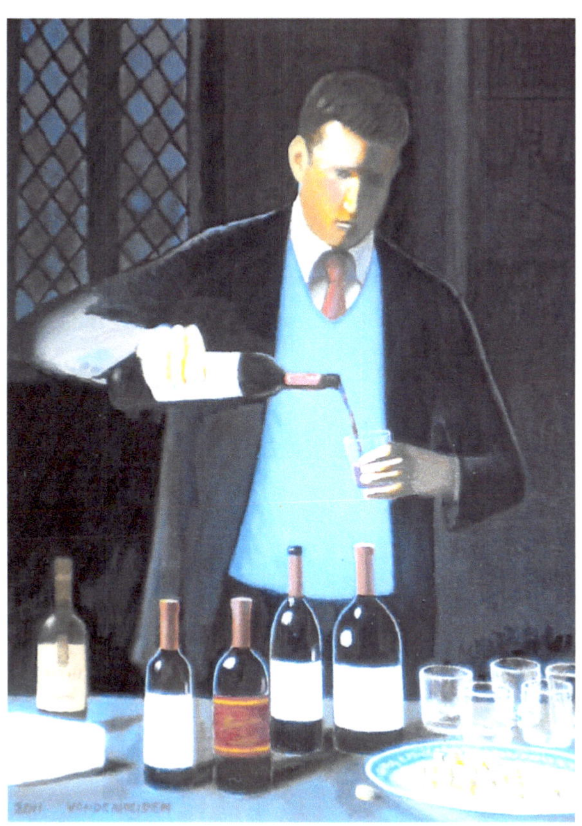

The Sommelier, 2011

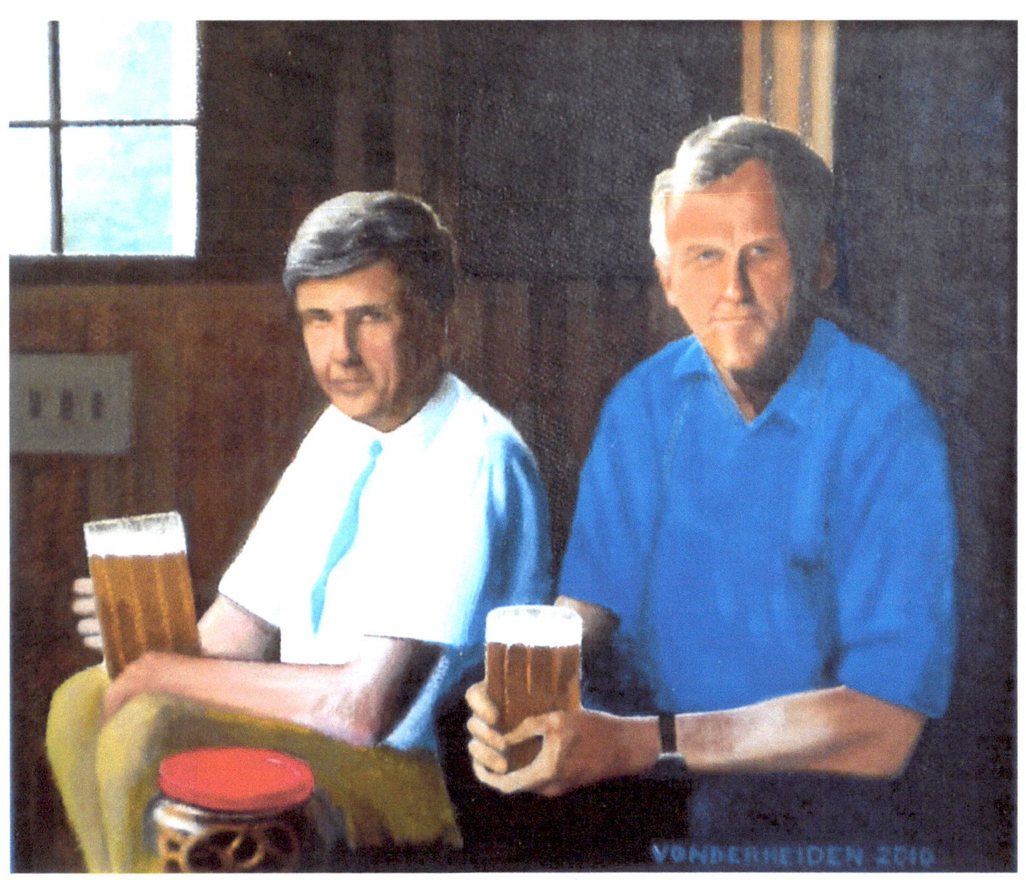

Pretzels & Beer (Bill Kraus & Walt Basler), 2010

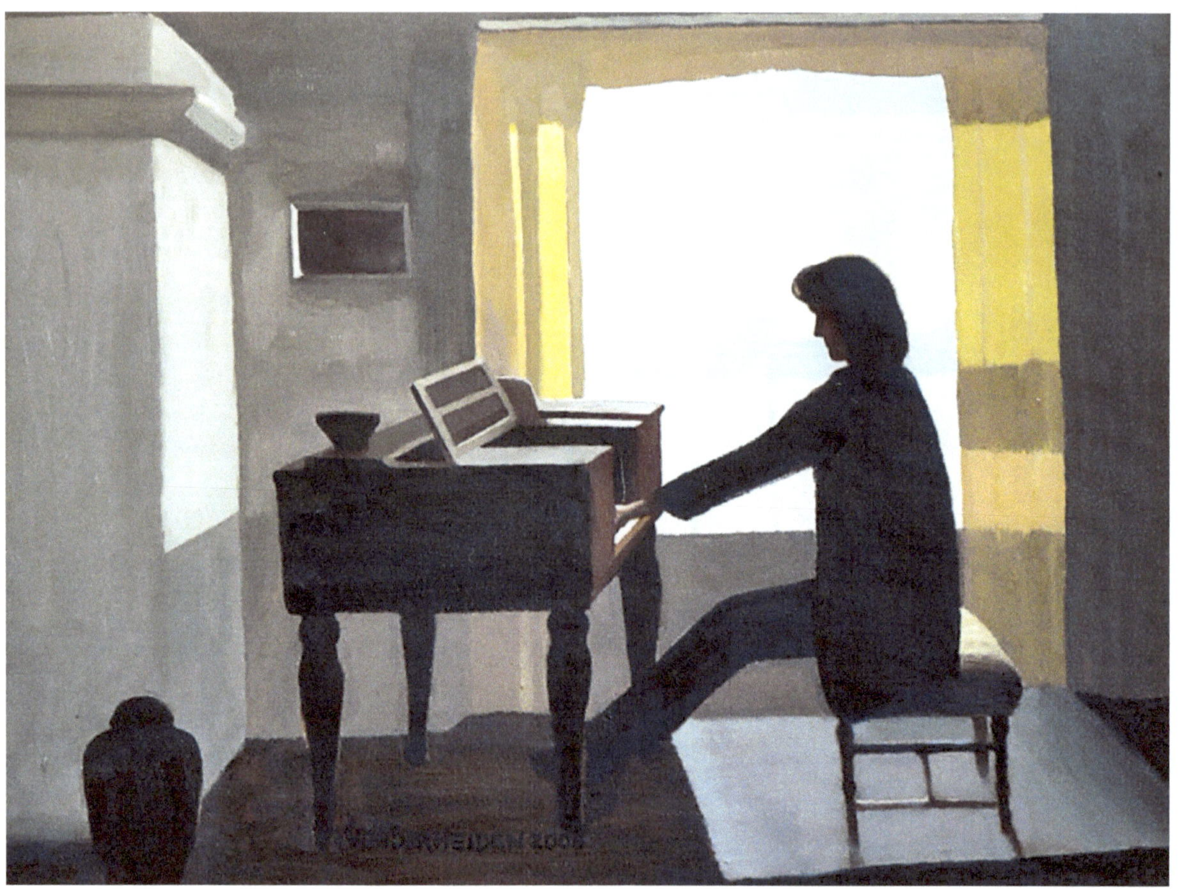

In the Piano Room, 2008

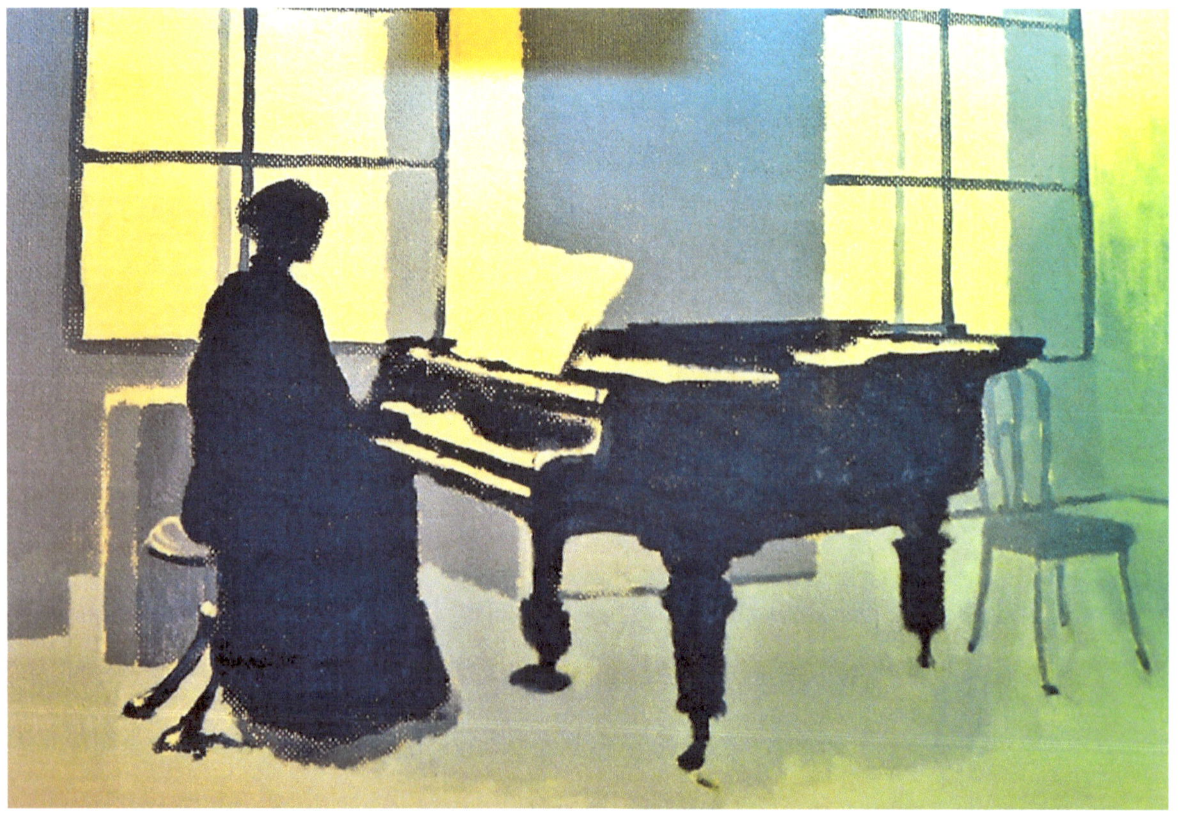

Another Piano Room (unfinished), 2008

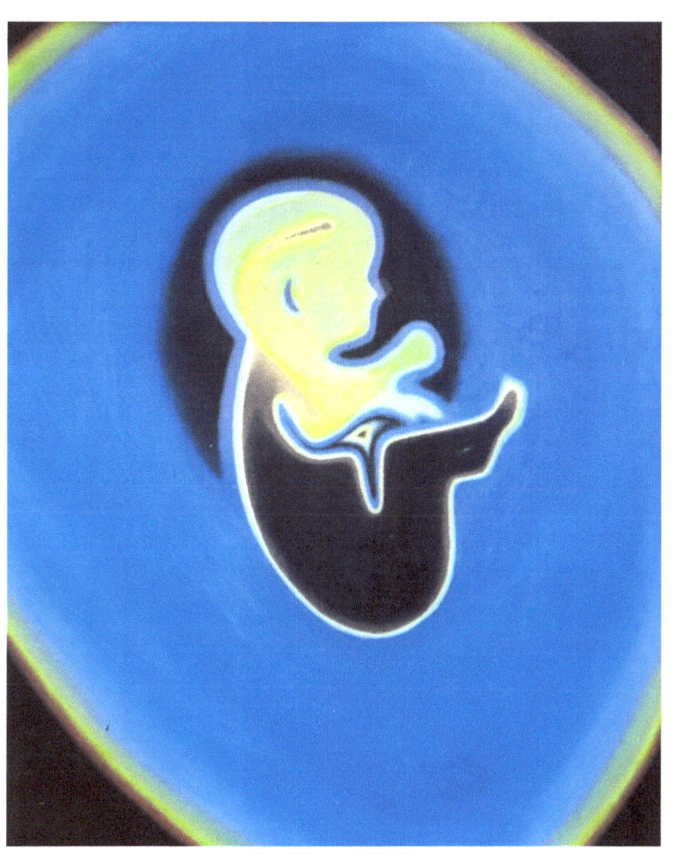

In Vivo, 2003

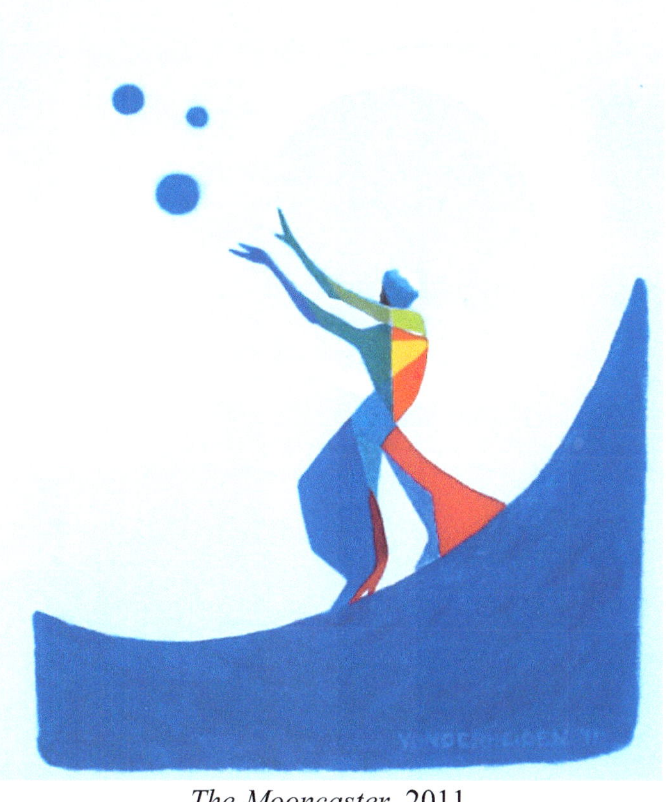

The Mooncaster, 2011

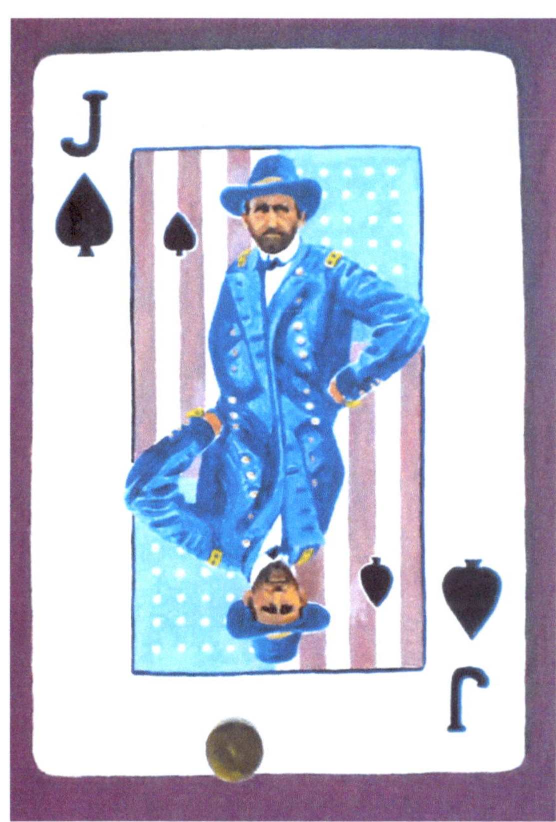

The Jack of Spades, 2012

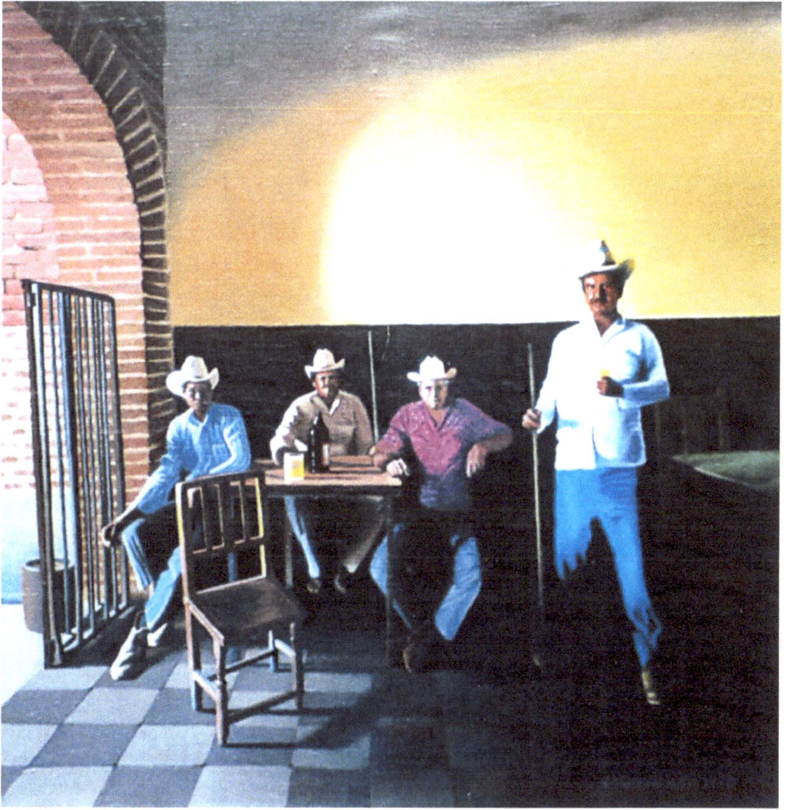

Amigos de Billar, 2008

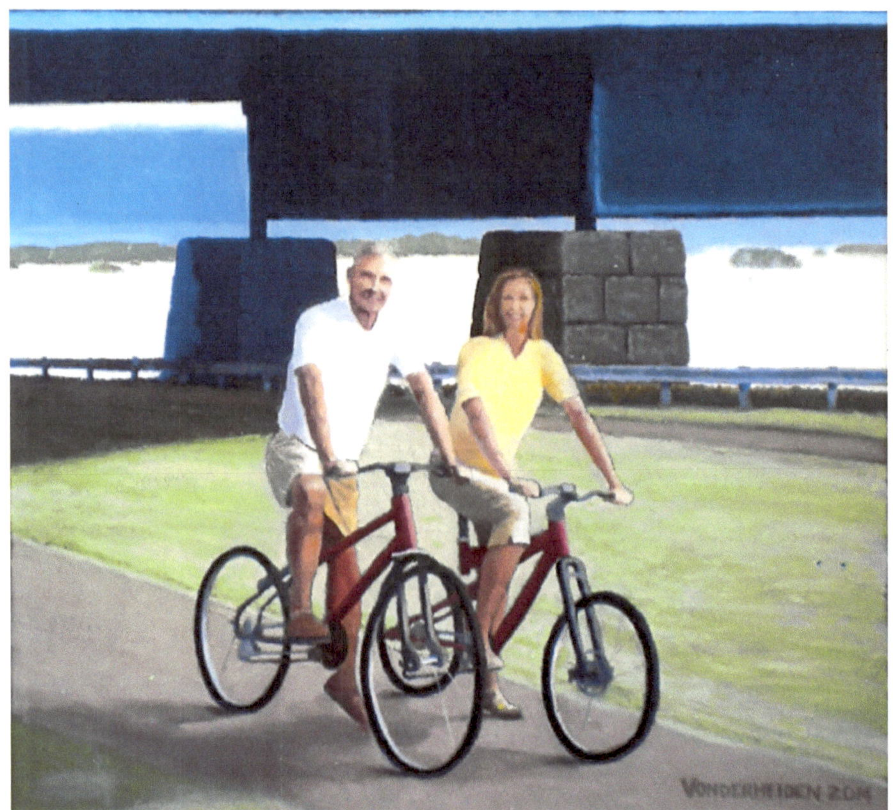

Pedalers by the Bridge Piers, 2014

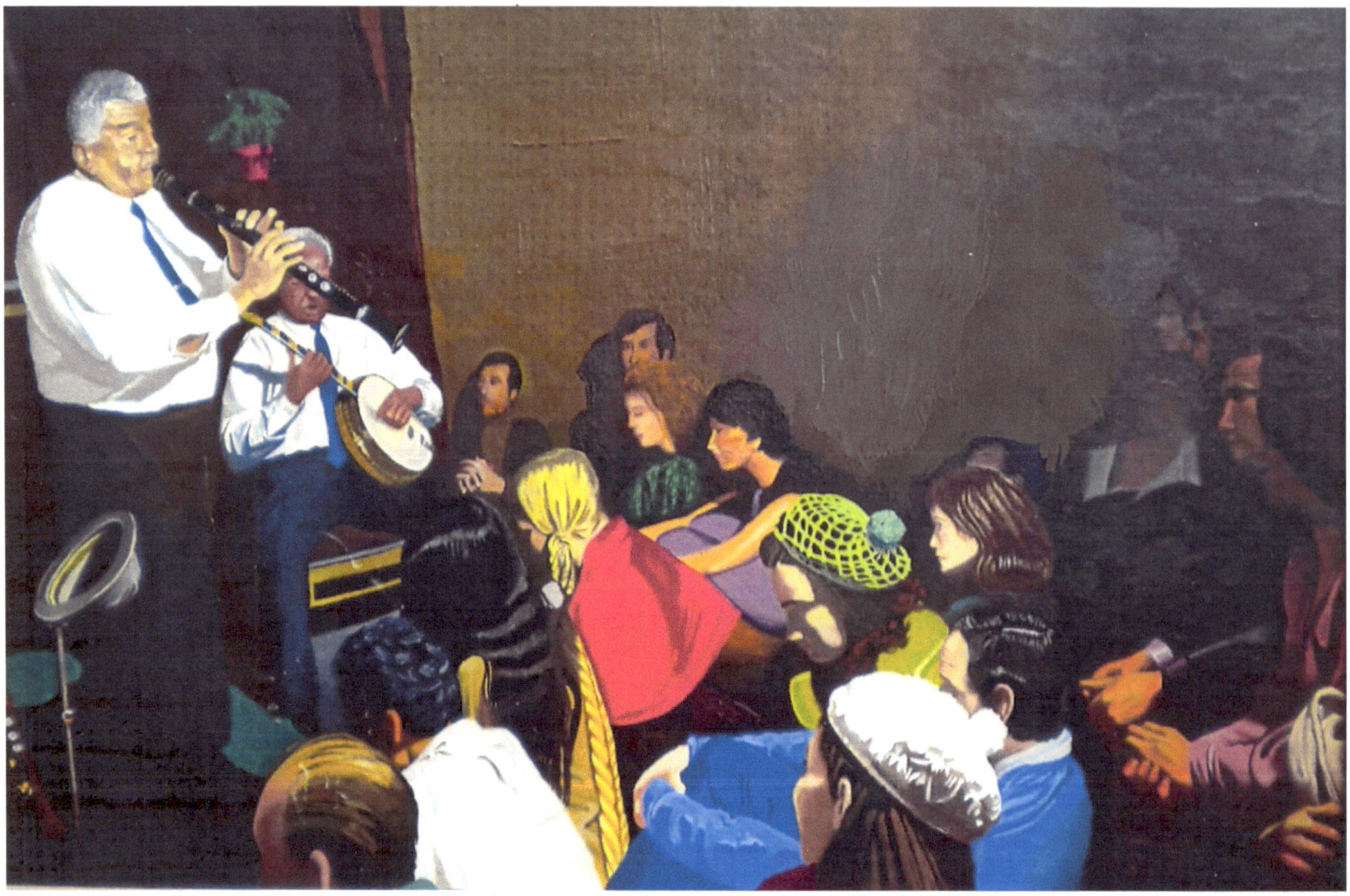

A Performance at Preservation Hall, 1970

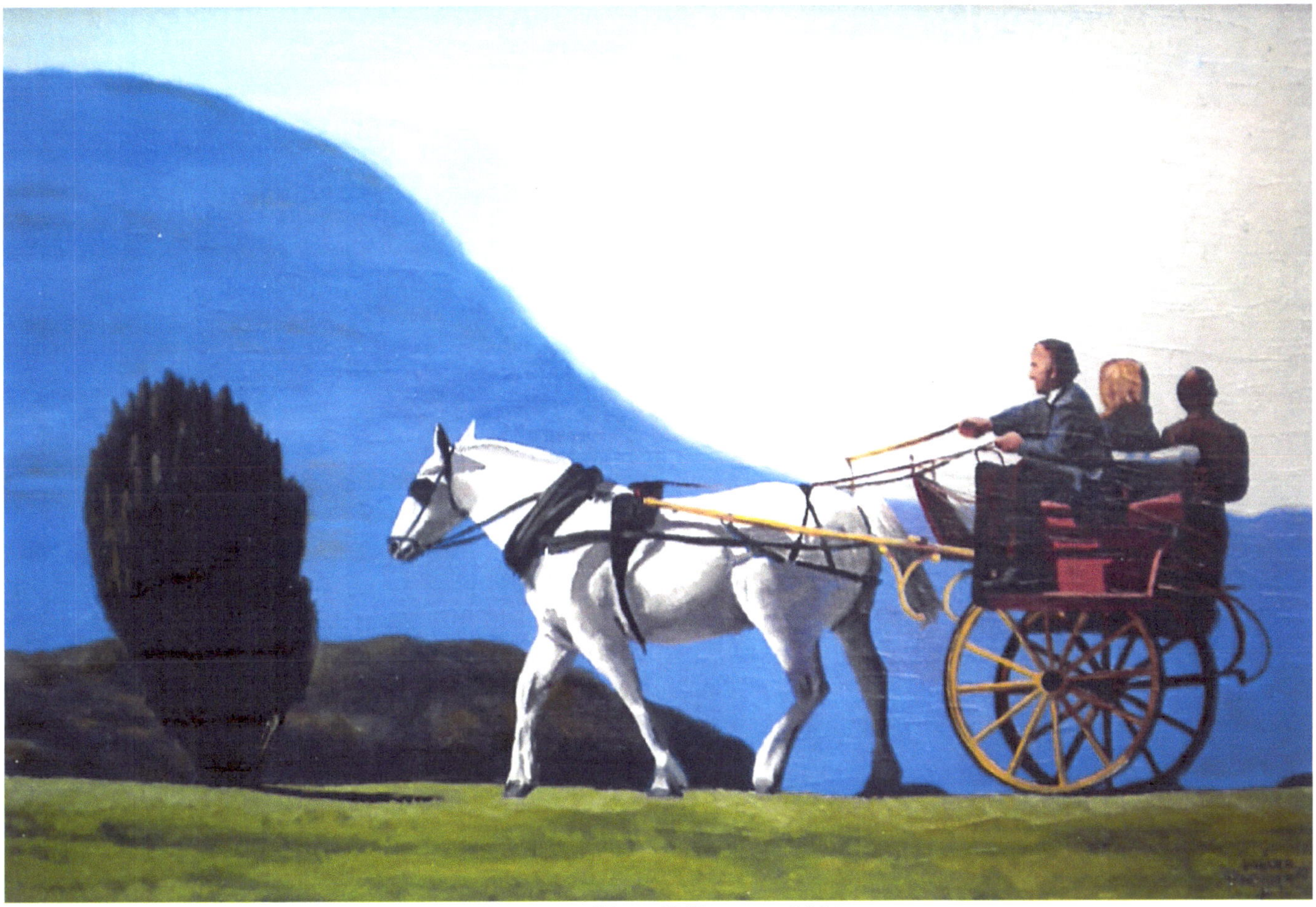

Jaunting Near Killarney, 1982

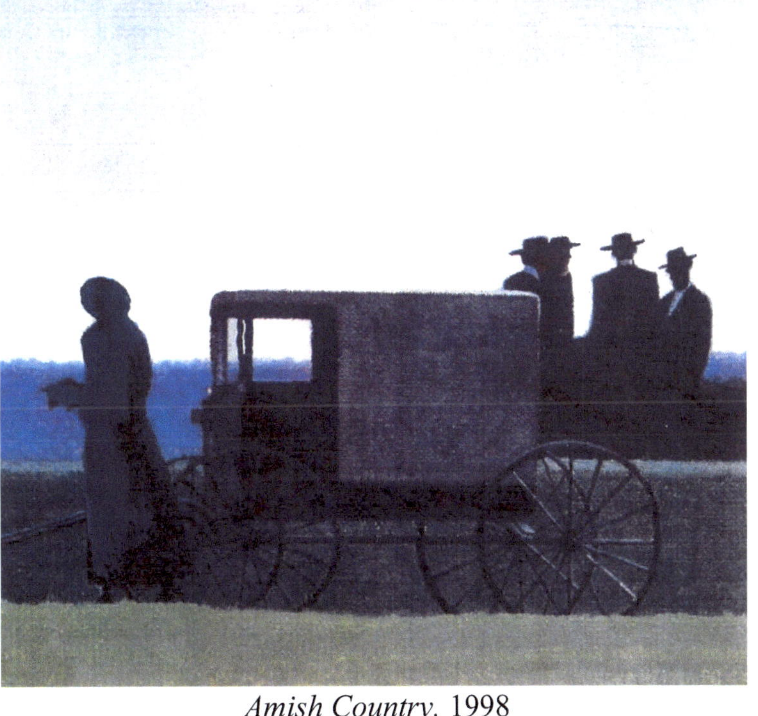

Amish Country, 1998

Landscapes and Lighthouses

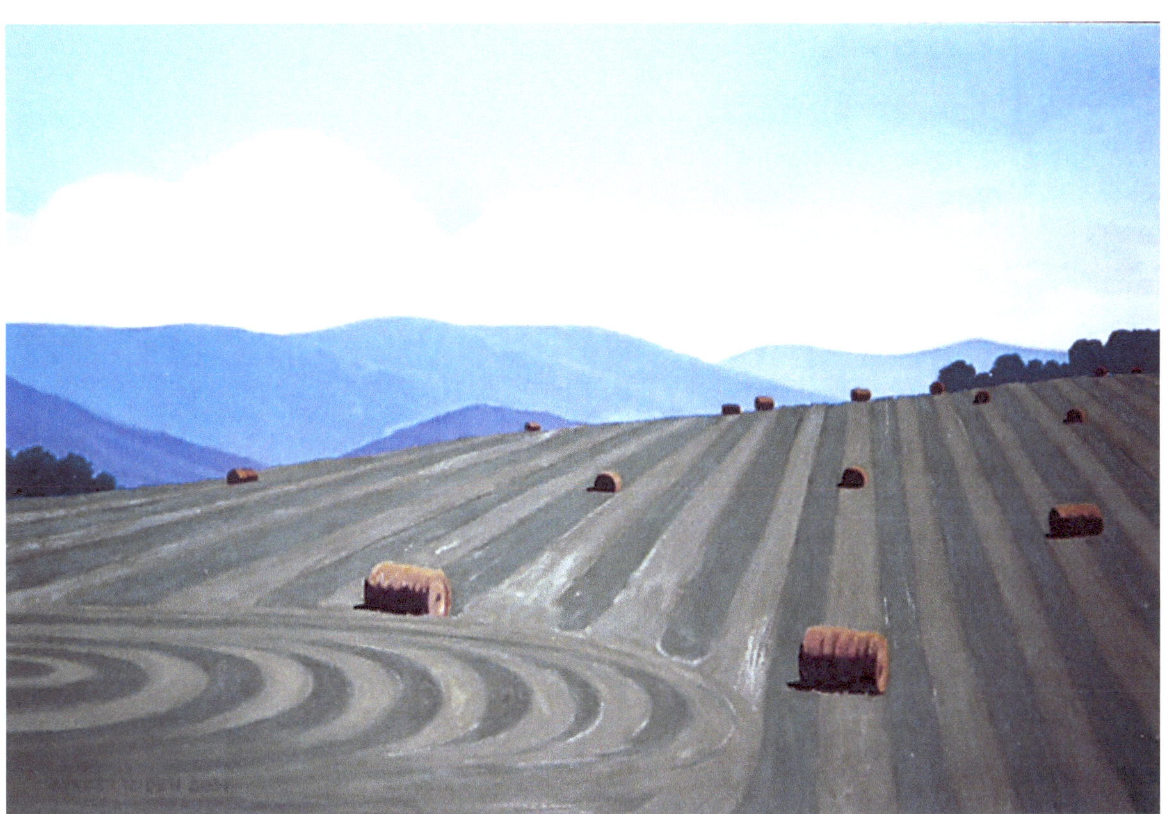

Hayrolls in Virginia, 2004

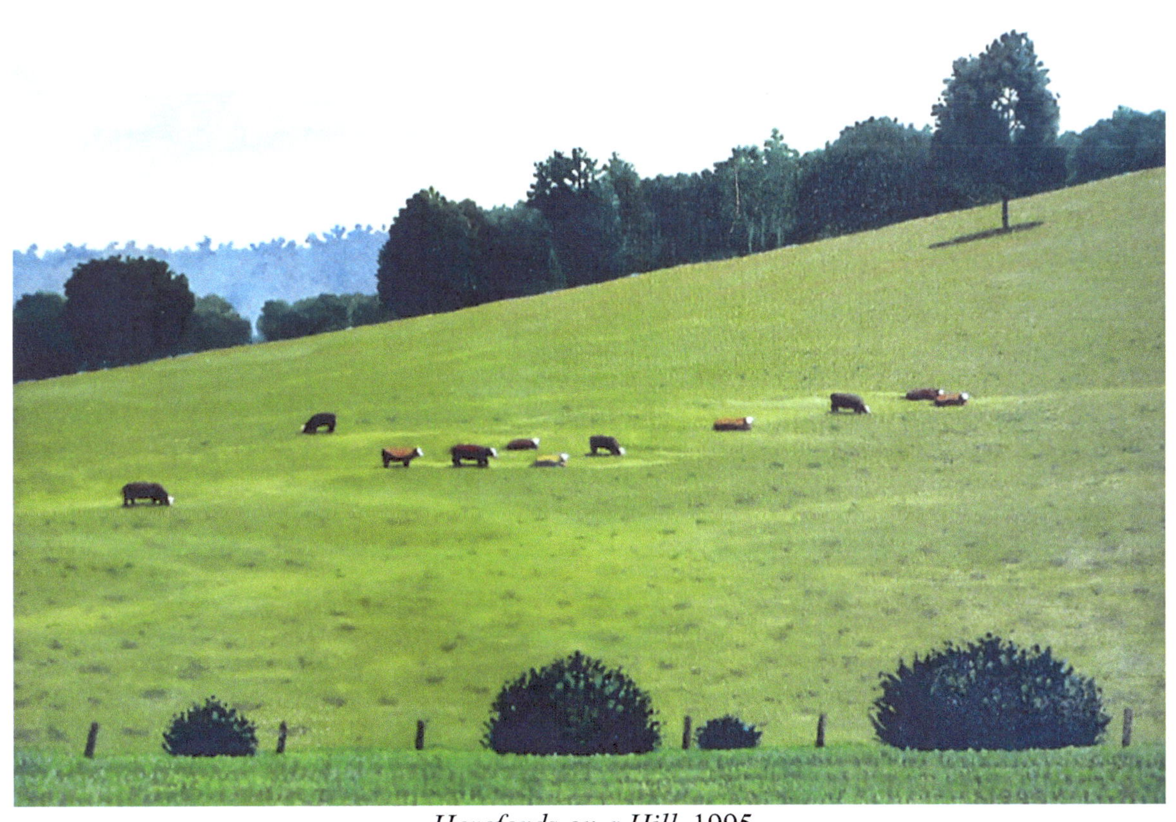

Herefords on a Hill, 1995

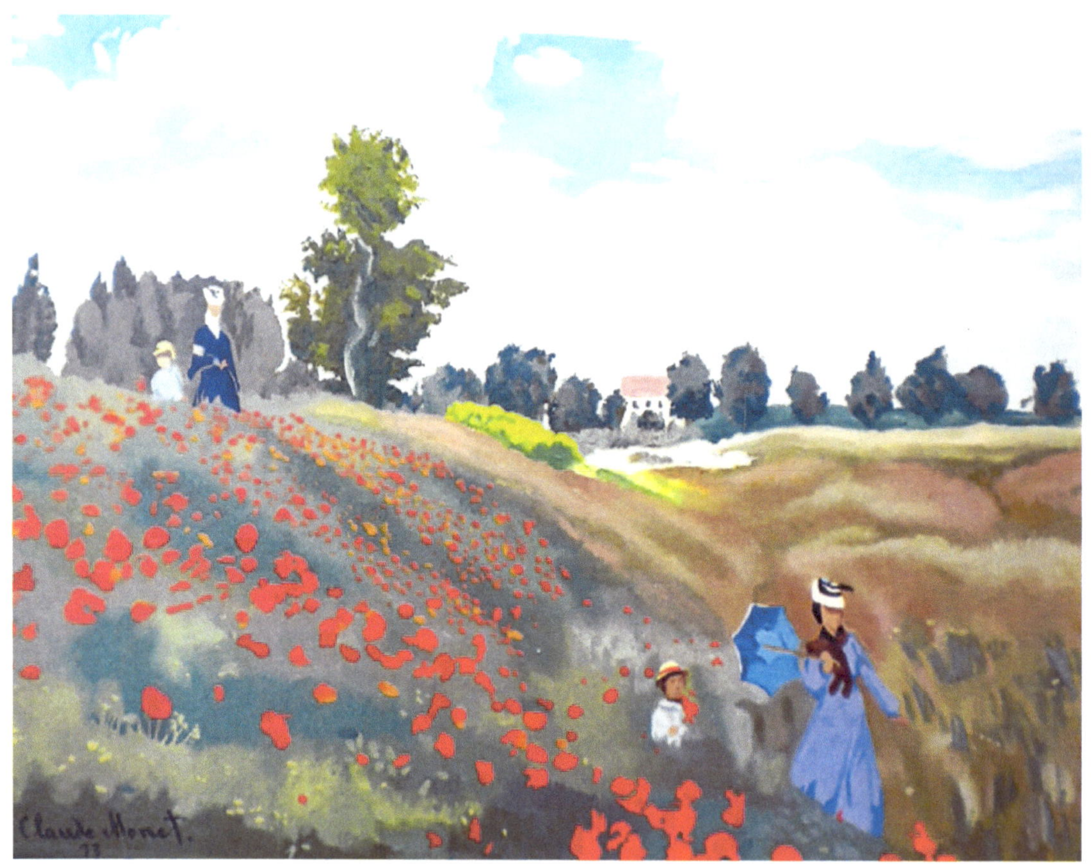

Field of Poppies (after Monet), 2002

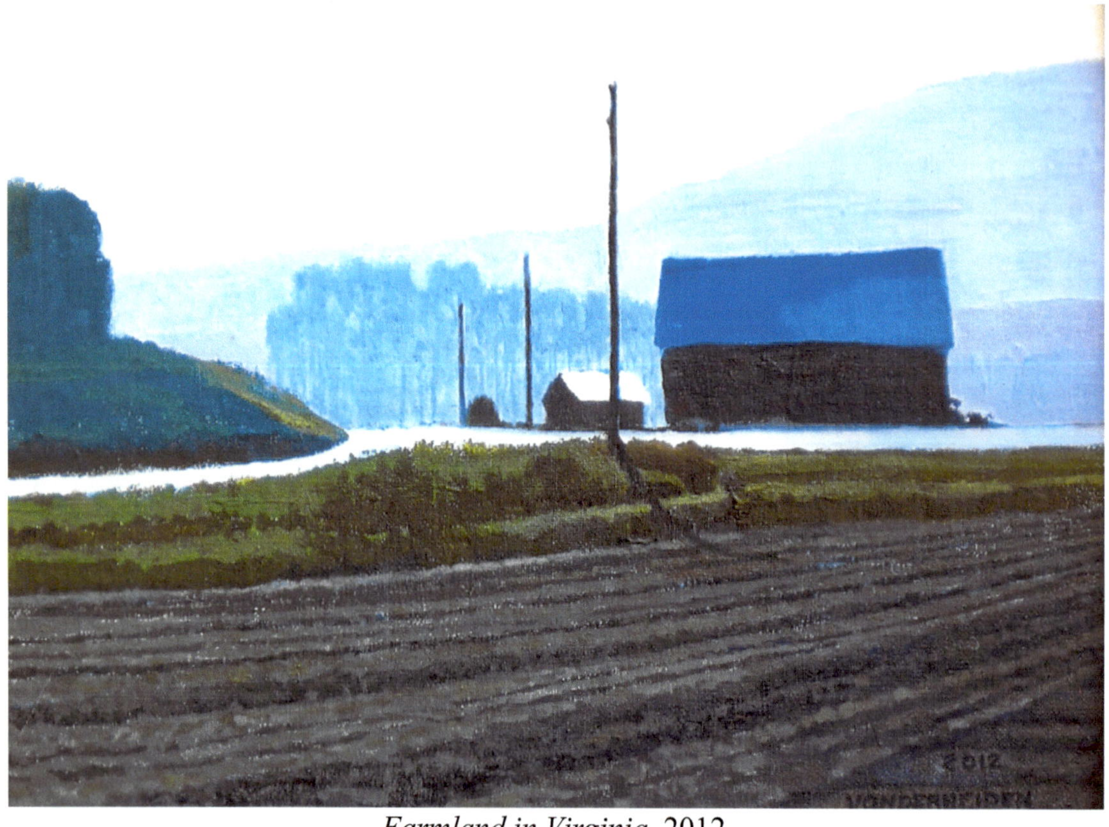

Farmland in Virginia, 2012

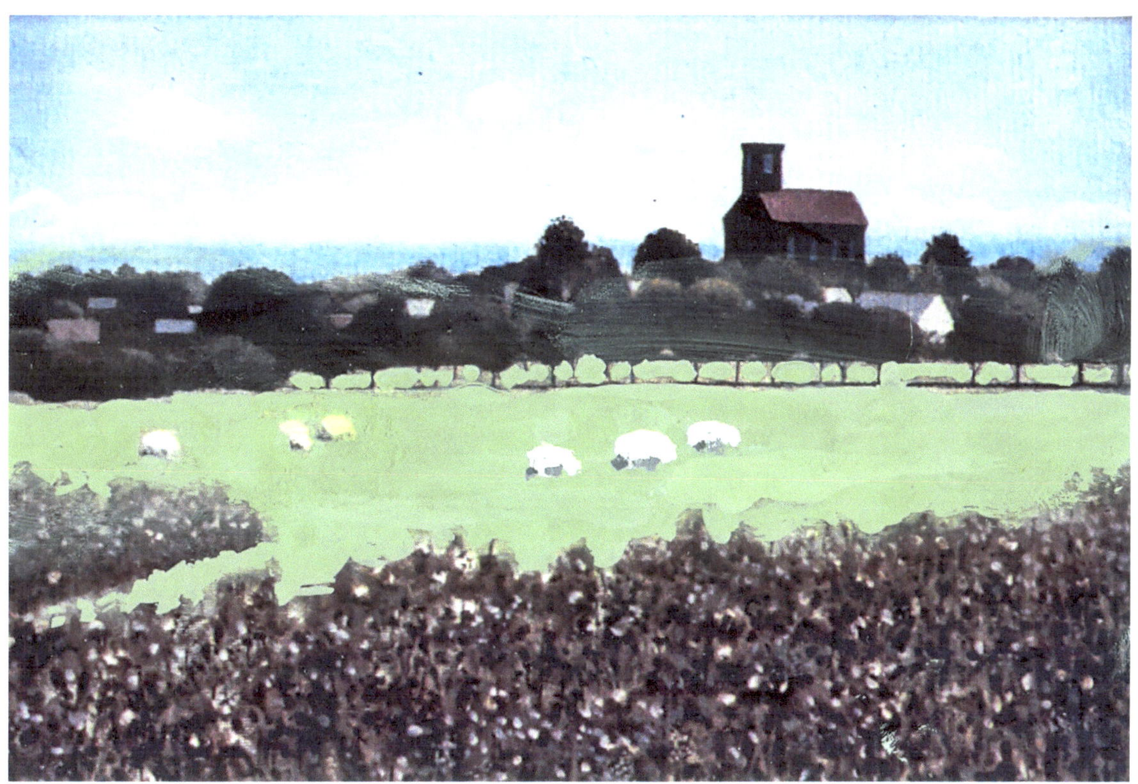

The Church at Shartlesville with Sheep, 1999

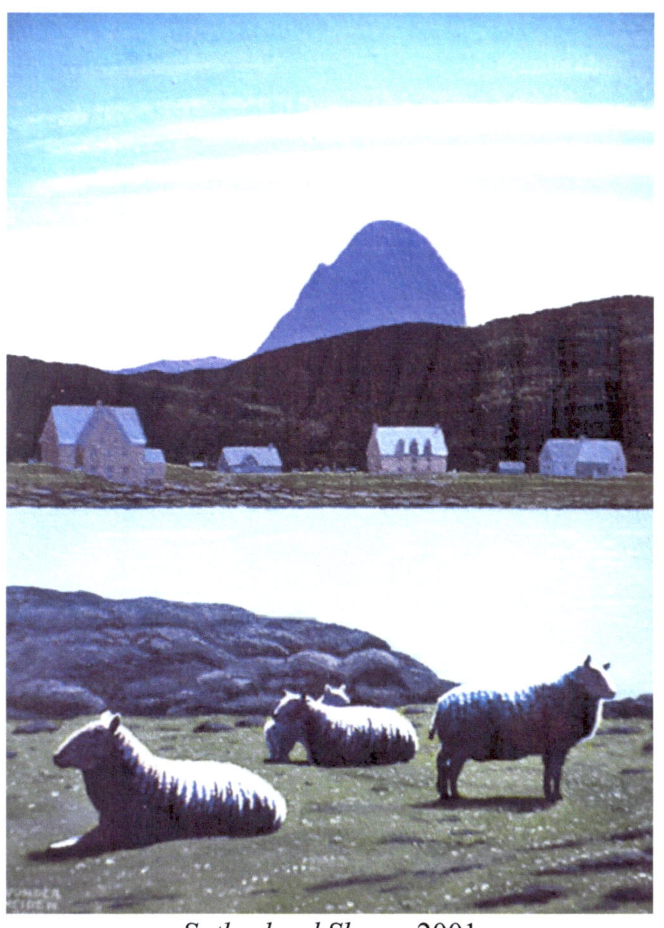

Sutherland Sheep, 2001

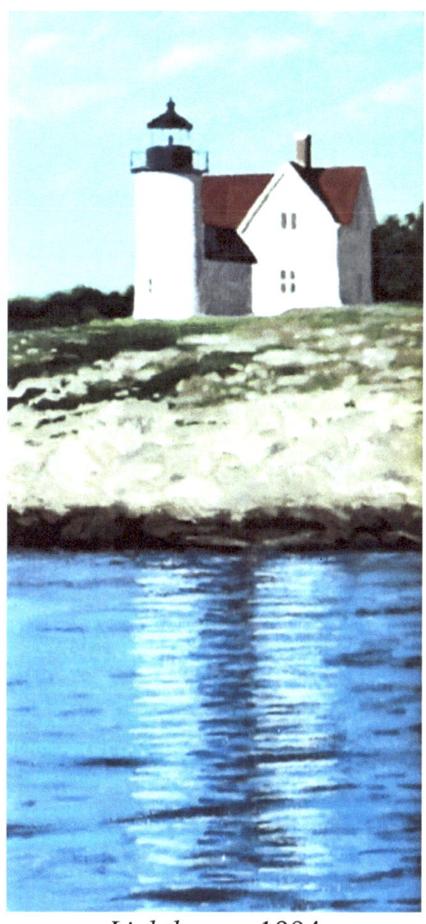

Lighthouse, 1994

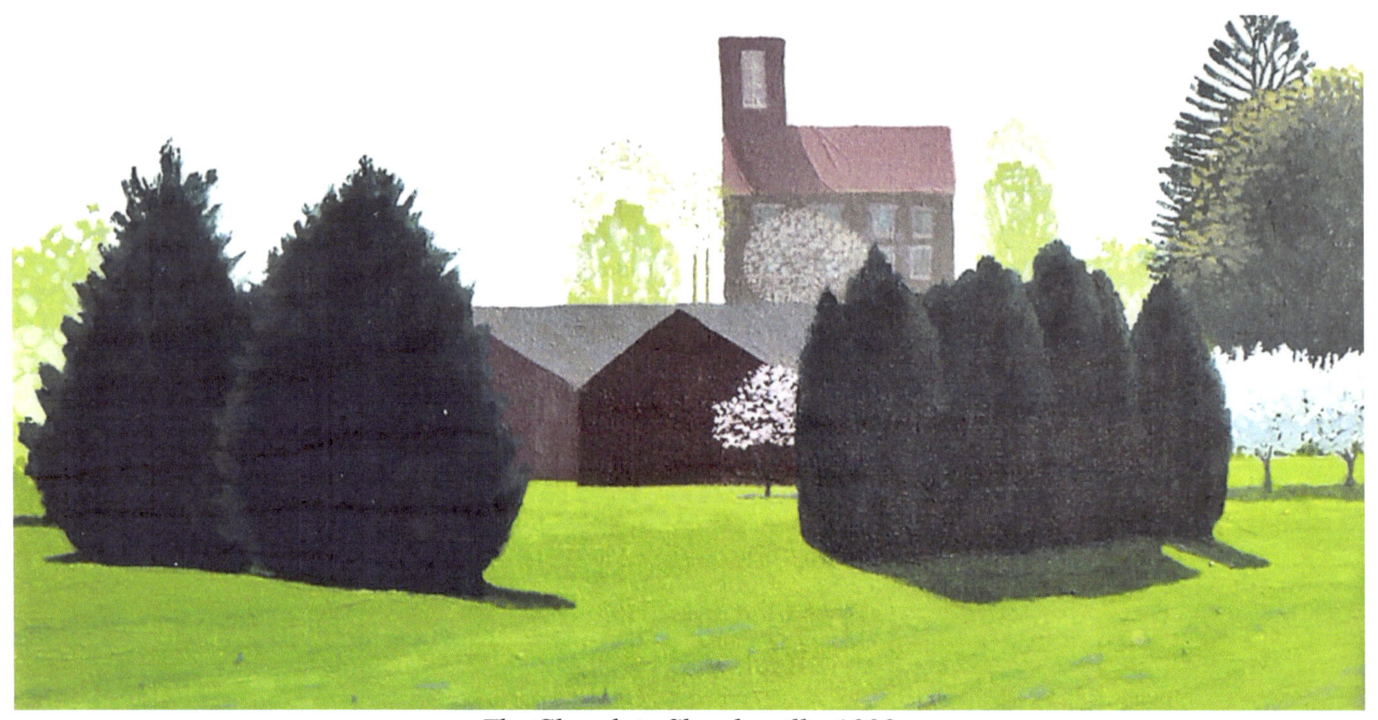

The Church in Shartlesville, 1998

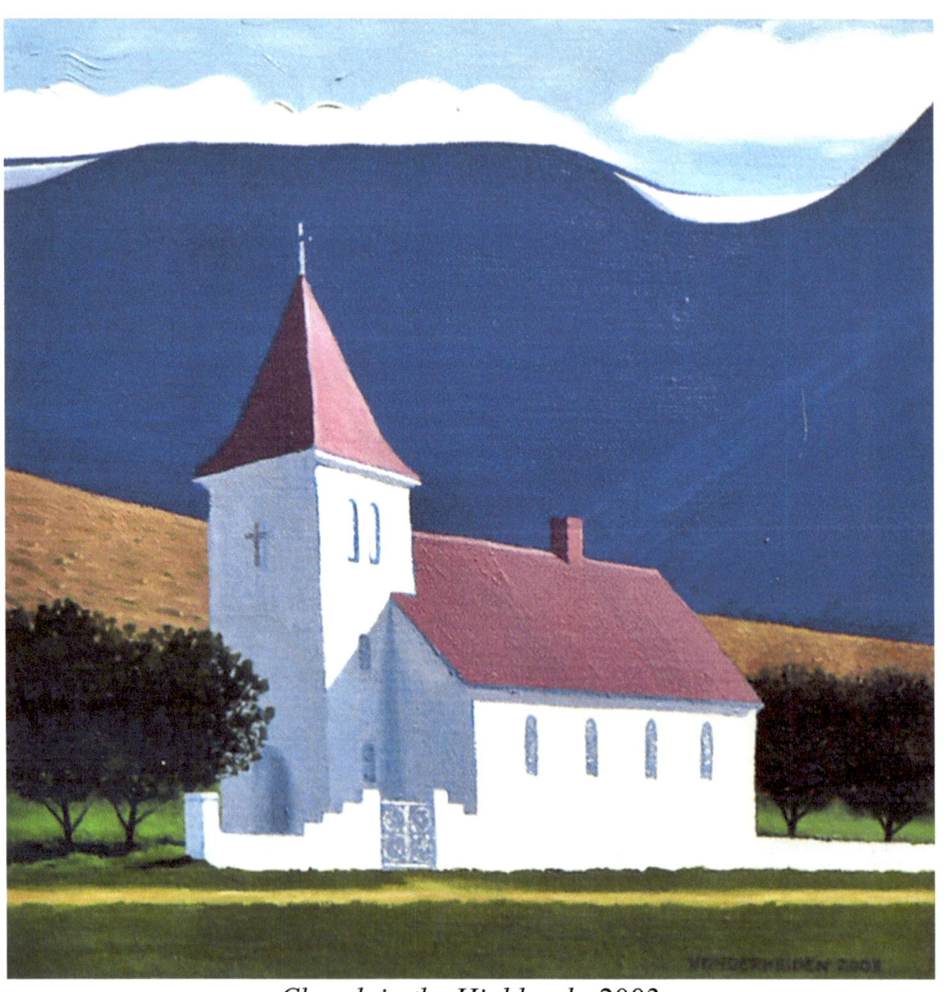

Church in the Highlands, 2003

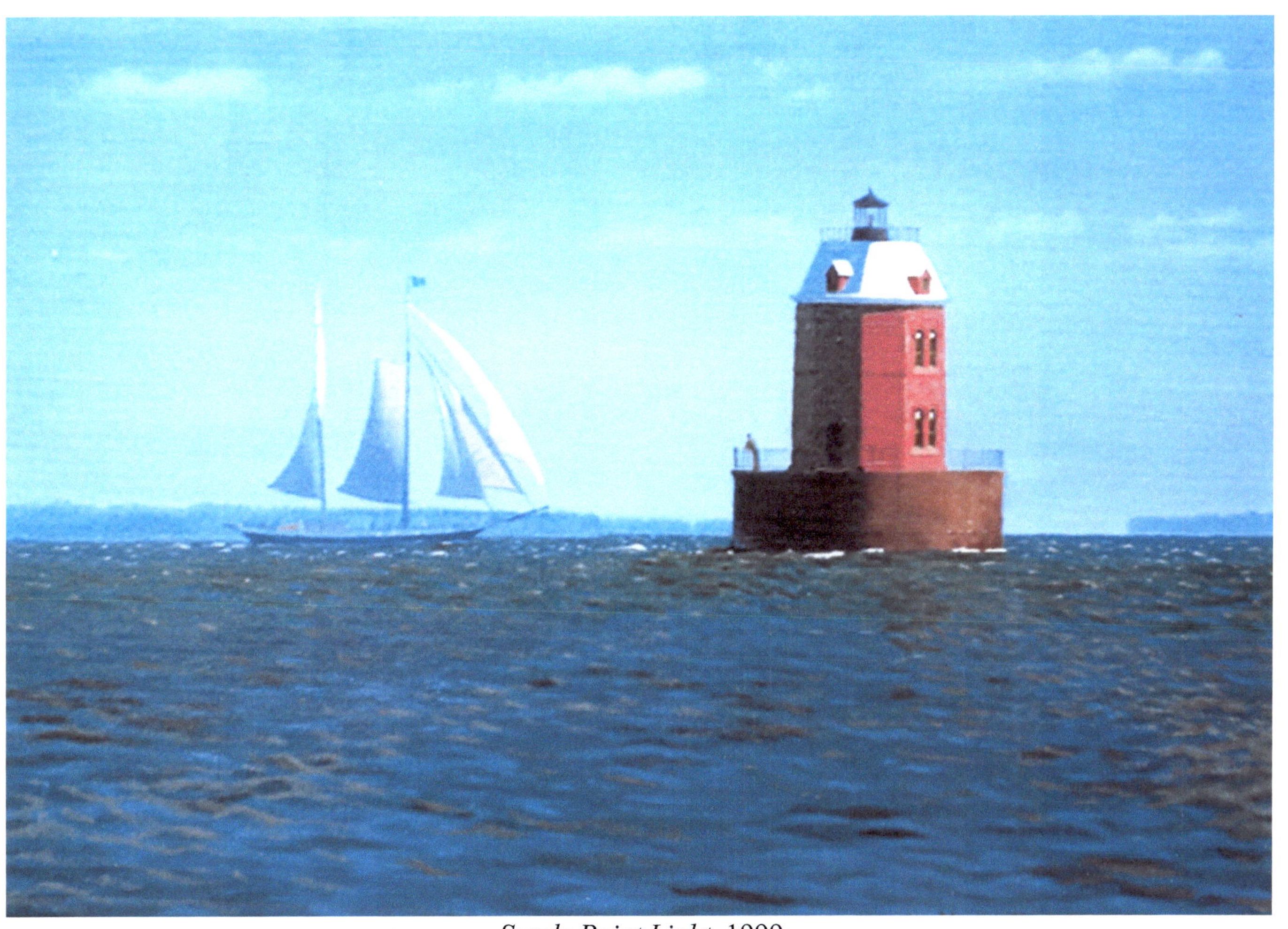

Sandy Point Light, 1999

Still Life and Wildlife

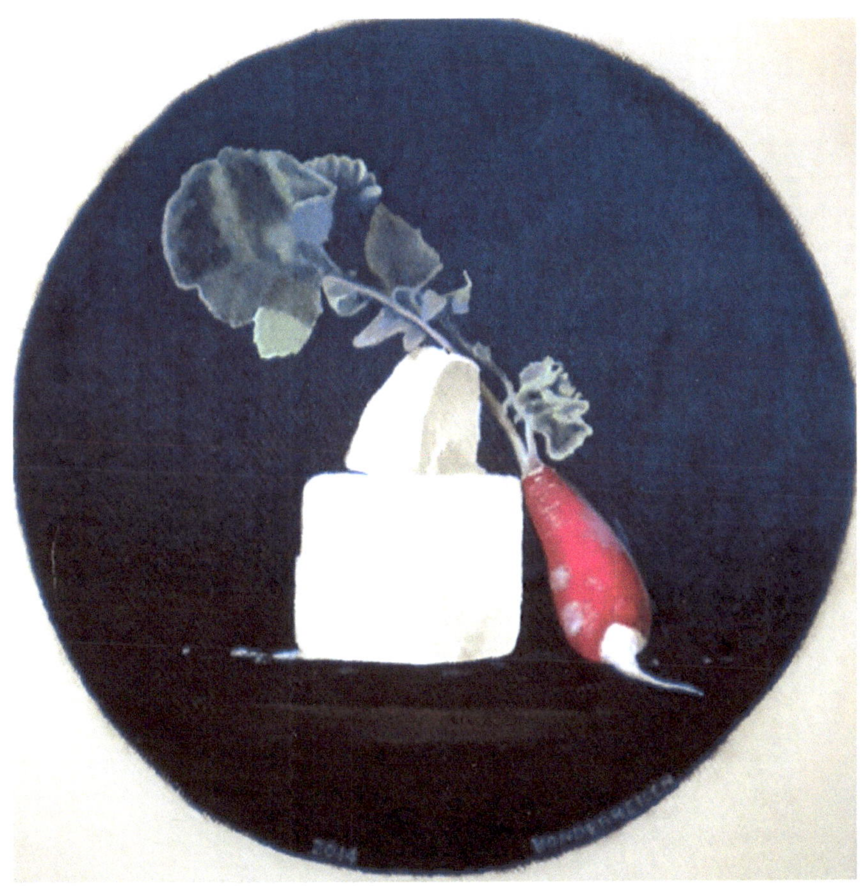

Cheese with a French Radish, 2014

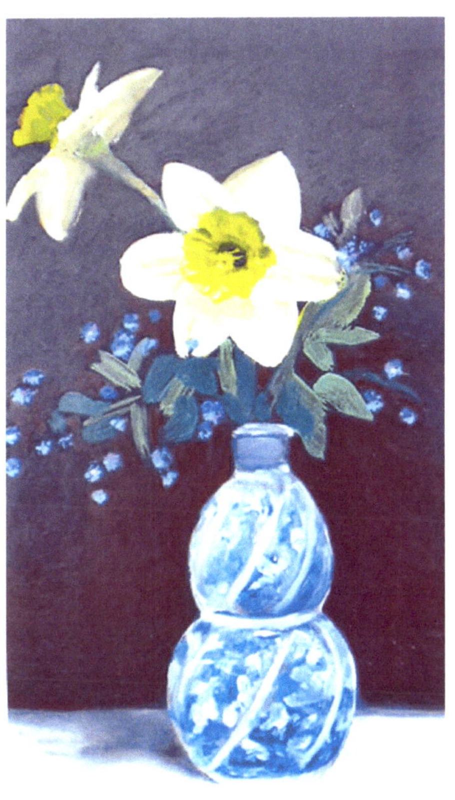

Blooms in a Blue Vase, 1978

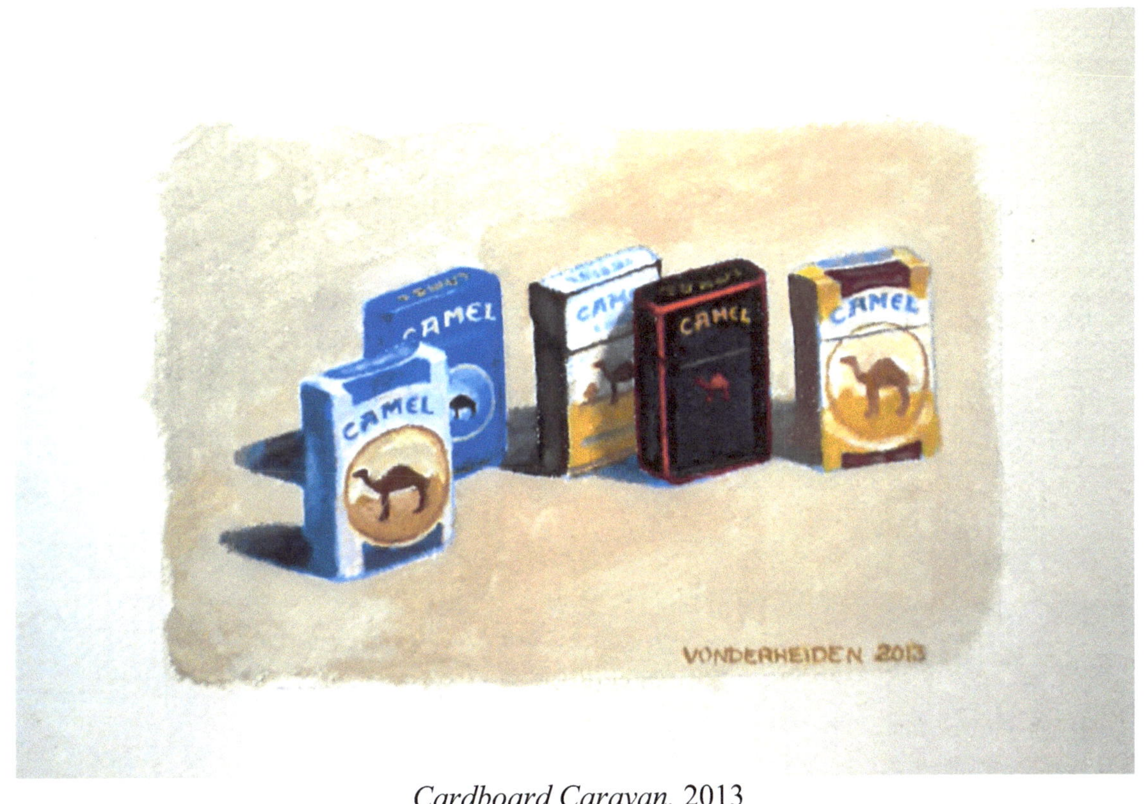

Cardboard Caravan, 2013

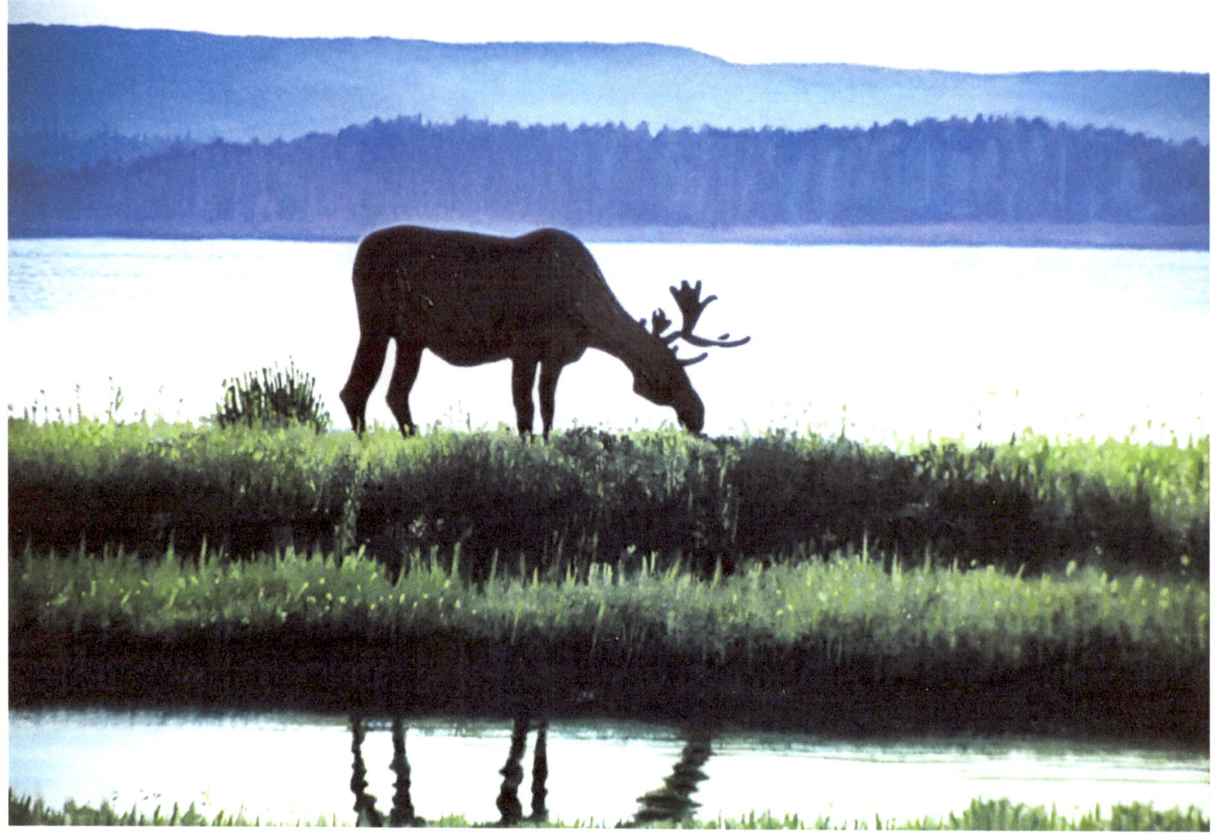

A Moose at the Lake, 1993

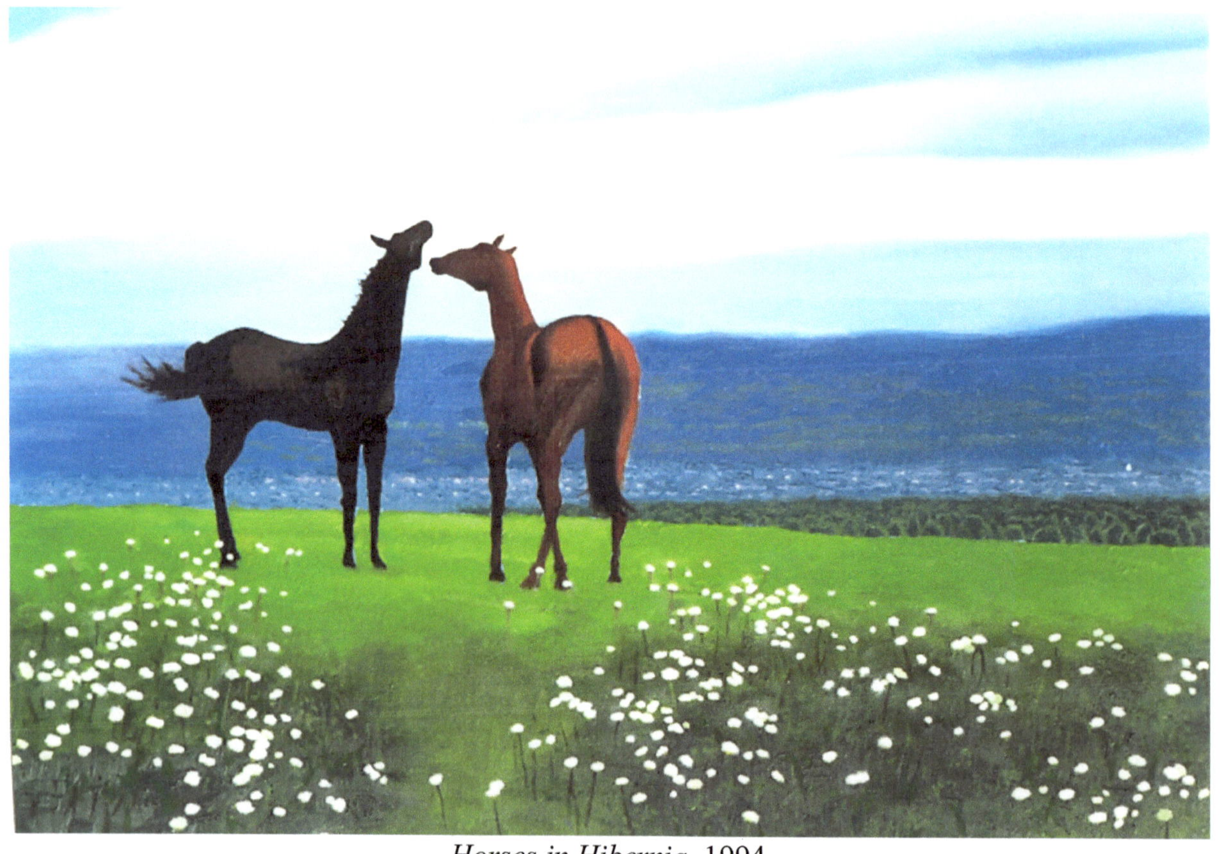

Horses in Hibernia, 1994

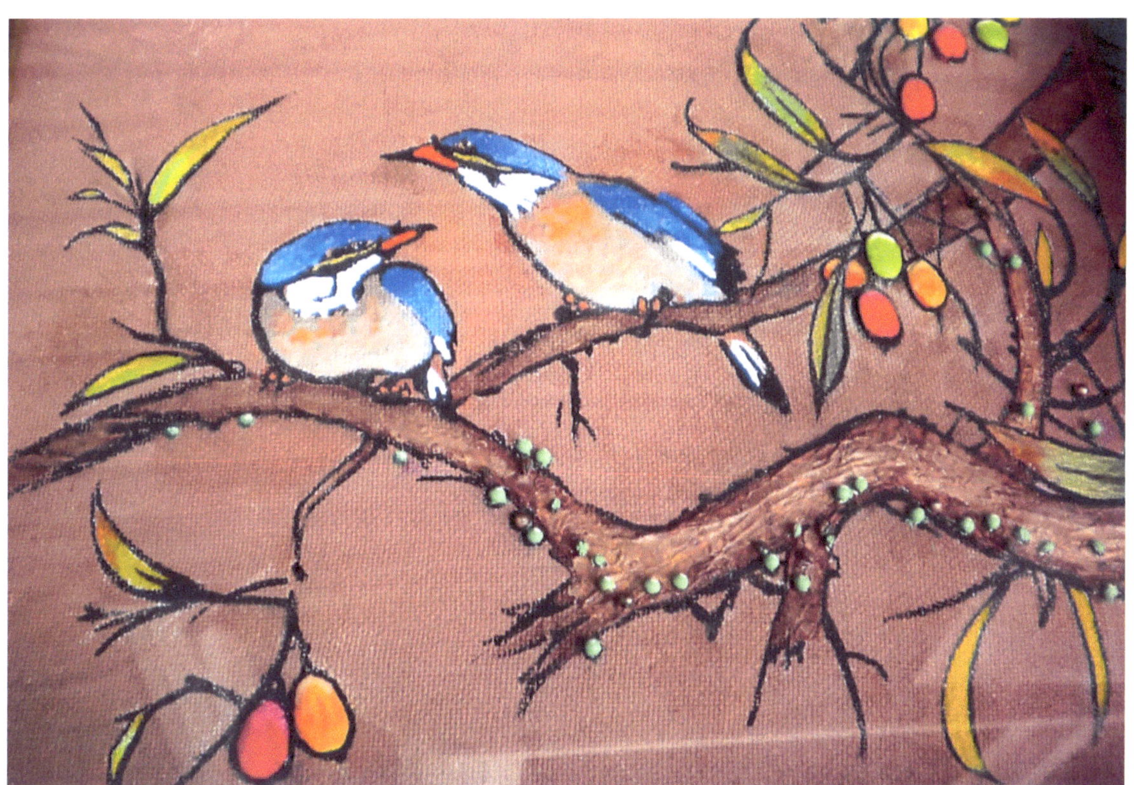

Birds in a Fruit Tree, 2012

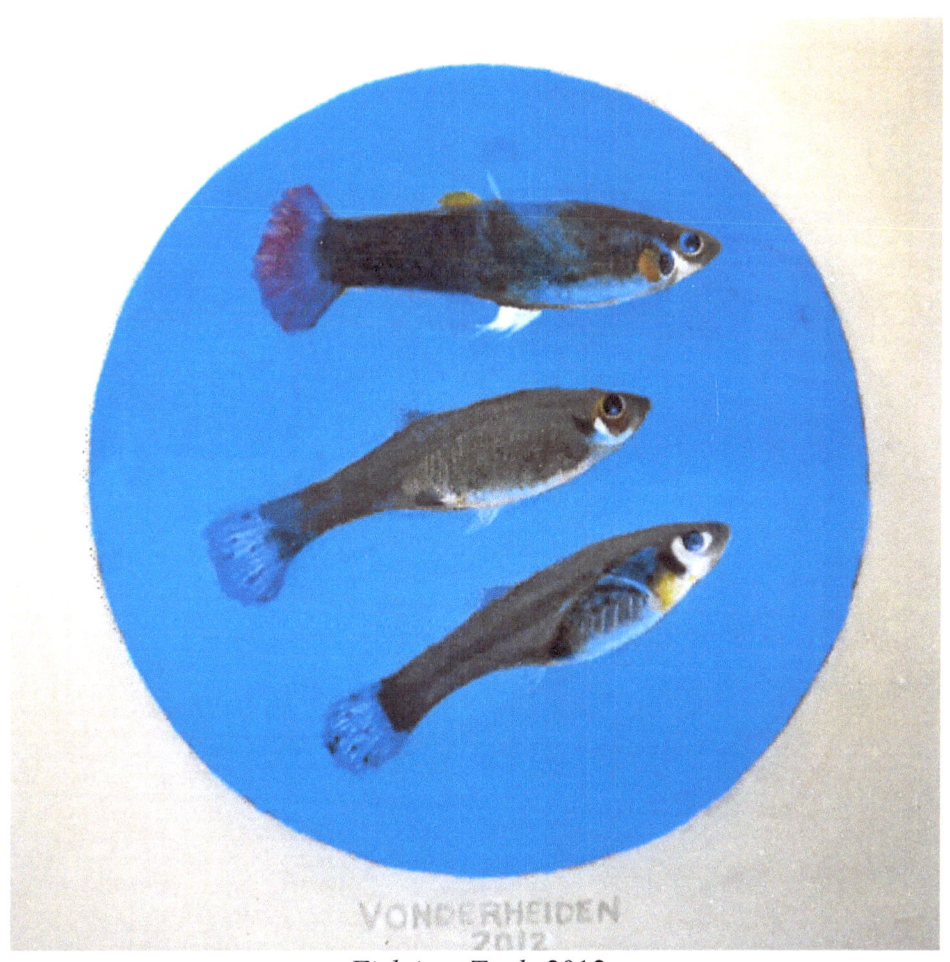

Fish in a Tank, 2012

www.ingramcontent.com/pod-product-compliance
Lightning Source LLC
LaVergne TN
LVHW070219110826
845147LV00003B/609

* 9 7 8 1 6 2 0 0 6 4 4 9 8 *